RICHARD DALY has been in full-time church ministry for the past twenty-seven years. During this time, he has pastored several churches in the West Country and within London. He has been involved in several mission projects in various parts of Africa including Ghana, Rwanda, Zimbabwe and Malawi. Pastor Daly has a passion for working within the community, and in doing so, has served in local community initiatives and leadership projects. He has extended his ministry as a hospital, prison and university volunteer chaplain and served at the London 2012 Olympic Games as a chaplain, ministering to athletes and personnel within the Olympic village.

Richard has authored fourteen books including the *God's Little Book* series. He is married to Maxine and together have three children. Outside of ministry, Richard enjoys playing tennis and squash.

CALM YOUR SOUL

A Year of Spiritual Tranquillity

RICHARD DALY

WILLIAM COLLINS

William Collins
An imprint of HarperCollins*Publishers*
1 London Bridge Street
London SE1 9GF

WilliamCollinsBooks.com

HarperCollins*Publishers*
Macken House, 39/40 Mayor Street Upper,
Dublin 1, DO1 C9W8 Ireland

First published in Great Britain in 2022 by William Collins

1

Printed and bound in the UK using 100% renewable electricity at CPI Group (UK) Ltd

This book is produced from independently certified FSC™ paper
to ensure responsible forest management

For more information visit: www.harpercollins.co.uk/green

This book was written mostly during the two years of lockdown during the coronavirus pandemic. It was a challenging time for many people. While some lost loved ones, others suffered severe symptoms which still have an impact to this day.

I dedicate this book to all those directly affected by the virus.

I also acknowledge those who are going through unsettling times – may the words on each page bring comfort and hope during the time in which we live today.

Avoid Emotional Burnout

It is not work that wears us out, but sadness, anxiety and worry. To God, all of your griefs are worthy of consideration.

The demands of life can be relentless. Each new day brings new challenges – finances, job insecurities, health concerns, family issues and personal problems, to name a few. How do we deal with the merry-go-round of life, trying to juggle several balls at once and still keep our feet on firm ground?

One thing that contributes to greater instability is holding on to the negative emotional baggage that often comes with life's toils. Worry, anxiety and sadness deplete the soul of necessary vital resources that keep it energised and sustained. You need to avoid that emotional burnout!

Casting your burdens on the Lord and leaving them there is the best way to rid yourself of each day's trials. Everything that concerns you is a concern to God – he's not too busy to want to help solve the small issues in your life.

FOR FURTHER REFLECTION

Philippians 4:6–7
1 Peter 5:7

Listen to Your Body

God in his ingenious, creative design, has built within us natural alarm signals – headaches, migraines, exhaustion, stress, agitation – to warn us when the pendulum of calm has swung too far in the wrong direction. Do yourself a favour and listen to your body.

If there's one voice that often gets squeezed out in the everyday journey of life, it's the voice of our own bodies. Our body speaks to us all the time about how it's feeling. Often we ignore that advice. When we push ourselves with overwork, overeating or anything that is in excess, our body screams for our attention: 'I'm tired – I need some rest!', 'My eyes are straining from being glued too long to that screen', 'I'm feeling dehydrated – I need some water!'

If we were to just take time to listen to our bodies, how much better we would feel on a daily basis! Our bodies would respond by saying 'Thank you for listening to me' and give us a much-needed feel-good factor. Respect your body and it will respect you!

FOR FURTHER REFLECTION

Psalm 32:8

Take Joy in Simplicity

The nicest and sweetest days are not necessarily those in which anything very spectacular or exciting happens, but those that bring simple pleasures – such as the sun sinking like a gold coin into the pocket of night.

We overcomplicate things in life. Running ahead of ourselves to reach a deadline or rushing to get somewhere on time means we lose out on so many simple things along the journey. Pace yourself. Give yourself room to pause and breathe. When you slow down you will start to notice things that have always been there. There are awesome, life-inspiring moments that occur almost every day, but we need to take time to notice them. So bring calm to your soul by appreciating those simple works of nature. Be inspired! Let nature speak to you of a God who is the perfect creator.

FOR FURTHER REFLECTION

Psalm 96:11–12

DAY 4

Let God Handle It

When you face an impossibility, leave it in the hands of the specialist. He won't necessarily handle it your way, but he'll handle it. 'The things which are impossible with men are possible with God.'

You can't do everything! Some things demand the expertise of a specialist. You may be able to solve some tasks, but you will always face impossible situations in life where you have no clue or idea how you will get through. Sometimes in those situations you may turn to God as the last resort, but don't leave him to the last minute when all the other doors have closed. Seek him first in every situation big or small – there's nothing he can't handle. If you allow him to handle the little things, you may find his method prevents anything becoming bigger.

FOR FURTHER REFLECTION

Luke 1:37
Luke 18:27

DAY 5

Be Anxious for Nothing

*Anxiety is debilitating. It weakens your
mental, emotional and physical capabilities.
Counteract it by replacing an anxious thought
with a biblical promise of strength.*

Contemplating nagging thoughts will wear you down. It draws more energy than you can imagine. The emotional and mental trauma of worry can deplete you of your natural resources. That's why the art of thought transfer is important. It's not that difficult. When a worrying thought enters your mind, counteract it with one of your favourite Bible promises. Over time an association develops with that worrying thought and you can be assured it will soon diminish in its influence and effects.

FOR FURTHER REFLECTION

Matthew 6:34

DAY 6

Trust Him Implicitly

You will know when you're trusting God.
There will be a sense of calm and serenity over the
situation that is giving you cause for concern.

What is the evidence that you are in the mode of trusting God? Simply put, you will have a sense of calm over you! You won't be limited in doing daily tasks like concentrating on your work, resting and eating meals. It's a beautiful feeling to experience, knowing that God will take care of the situation.

FOR FURTHER REFLECTION

Psalm 23:4

DAY 7

Breathe Slowly

In times of nervousness or panic, your metabolism
speeds up, powered by a palpitating heart.
Take control of your breathing by dictating the pace.

Nervous reactions can run riot over your body. However, you don't have to be incapacitated by these impulsive reactions. Clear your mind by taking long, deep breaths. Exhale your tensions away and inhale calm. Take a deep breath and exhale tension, now inhale calm. Do this several times, like breathing in deep fresh air on a new morning. You will find the body will follow suit by slowing down. You can dictate the pace!

FOR FURTHER REFLECTION

Psalm 62:1–2
Psalm 65:5

DAY 8

Bask in the Sunshine

The rays of the sun have 'healing in their wings'.
Enjoying a few moments of natural sunlight creates
necessary nutrients for well-being which triggers
a positive feel-good factor.

In the cold and dark days of the late autumn and winter months, our only desire is to get home and stay inside. However, while we are warm and snug at home, we are missing vital nutrients that can only be obtained through natural sunlight. We may not feel the warmth of the sun in cold seasons, but the rays of the sun when they do peek out still have remedial benefits. Find a way to catch this healing balm of sunlight!

FOR FURTHER REFLECTION

Malachi 4:2

Claim Christ's Forgiveness

Jesus' first words on the cross were a prayer:
'Father, forgive them, for they do not know what they do.'
The 'them' includes you. Claim his forgiveness and
release yourself from any past guilt and shame.

When Christ was dying on the cross his only thought was of you and me. He died to save humanity from the impending effects of sin by taking our place. For that sacrifice to be complete, we had to be forgiven from our sins. That's what Christ managed to do – even as he was dying he was interceding for us. When you consider all Christ did for you, all he wants in return is for you to accept that forgiveness. That means believing all your past sins are no longer on your head!

FOR FURTHER REFLECTION

Luke 23:34

Release Control

Trusting God involves being willing to let go.
That means no longer trying to control your situation
or circumstances. When you've become vulnerable
to God, you experience true security in him.

We like to be in control. It's a safety buffer that's inbuilt within us to ensure we survive. While it may be necessary for us to protect ourselves from harm or danger through this inbuilt mechanism, it sometimes extends to other areas of our lives and inhibits us from trying new things or coming out of our comfort zones. We then become too overprotective. Being open and vulnerable with God is relinquishing that control, letting God have free access and allowing him to take the steering wheel of your life.

FOR FURTHER REFLECTION

Proverbs 3:5–6

You Can't Do Everything

*Acknowledging your limitations will go a
long way towards helping you to learn to say no.
Leave the heroism to God and let him take the credit.*

There's something about wanting to please other people that makes us go above and beyond our capabilities. Yes, it's a good thing to help others, but we have to know our limits. When we take on something that's too demanding, what is the real motive? Is it to seek recognition or credit for the task? Sometimes it's better to support that person by directing them to the God of all things who can do all things.

FOR FURTHER REFLECTION
Jeremiah 45:5

DAY 12

Praise Your Way to Calm

Being thankful and expressing that through
praise dispels nagging negative thoughts and feelings.
Praising God reminds you who is the source and
sustainer of your life.

We like to receive praise from other people. It's a natural desire, especially when we have put a lot of effort into a task or gone out of our way to do something big. There's absolutely nothing wrong in receiving praise, it's how we respond to it that counts. When we praise God, however, we take the attention away from ourselves to the one who completely deserves it. Praise can range from a simple prayer of thanks to a full-blown, hand-raising dance session in the privacy of your front room! Either way, it's all geared towards God.

FOR FURTHER REFLECTION

Psalm 100:4–5
Isaiah 25:1

DAY 13

Remember, You're Amazing!

God says you are 'the apple of his eye'.
He created and designed you as unique and
highly favoured. What God thinks of you is more
important than what others think of you.

It's nice to be adored. It's an act of love not everyone receives in life. You may not have a special friend who showers you with adoration or, worse still, adoration is not forthcoming from the special friend you do have! However, you have to believe the Bible when it says that God pours his heart out to you in love. He means it when he says you are special. Because of his ability to focus on you uniquely, be assured those adoring words are as though they are meant only and especially for you!

FOR FURTHER REFLECTION

Psalm 17:8
Jeremiah 1:5

DAY 14

Taste and See

The true worth of anything is having experienced it for yourself. To know God is to experience him, and to enjoy all the benefits that relationship brings.

Simply having a knowledge of God is not going to transform you. That belief has to impact how you feel. This in turn will affect how you behave. When you have an experiential relationship with God then you can see him for who he really is. It's a relationship that no one can challenge you on because it's borne from your own experience.

FOR FURTHER REFLECTION

Psalm 34:8

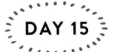

Come unto Me

The greatest invitation by Christ is to draw near to him with all our cares, worries and anxieties and replace them with the rest he has to offer. This rest extends to the total person, encompassing our physical, mental, emotional and spiritual dimensions.

There are some invitations we can turn down – the office party, a dinner date, a concert or even an all-you-can-eat buffet! But when someone offers you the opportunity to transfer all your worries, problems and issues onto them for free, ridding you of all the complexities and headaches that come with them, would you honestly want to turn that down? I wouldn't and I haven't. The good news is this invitation extends to everyone including you. So do yourself a favour today and get down to some offloading!

FOR FURTHER REFLECTION

Matthew 11:28

DAY 16

Consider the Little Things

*'Each little flower that opens, each little bird
that sings, he made their glowing colours, he made
their tiny wings.' 'All things' are still 'bright and
beautiful'. This well-known hymn, written by
C. F. Alexander, reminds us of the nuances
of God's perfect creation.*

Nature truly testifies to an amazing, creative God. Although we see many troubling developments today – inept attempts at effective conservation, endless pollution, destruction of forests and increasing carbon emissions to name but a few – there are still signs of God's amazing creation. Get out somewhere to bask in God's nature and allow it to remind you of the kind of God you serve.

FOR FURTHER REFLECTION

1 John 1:3

DAY 17

Compensate Yourself

When you overdo things, it's your body that usually suffers. Make up for that expended energy by restoring the body through rest, play or anything rejuvenating.

Your body deserves to be respected. It's always been there for you, working overtime, giving extra time and sometimes going to extreme limits for you. It wants to support and be there for you, but it's human. It needs to be appreciated. It has feelings and needs to be listened to. So do yourself a favour and treat it kindly. Let it have ample rest, and then let it play and laugh with you and it will be restored to serve you afresh for the next day!

FOR FURTHER REFLECTION

Proverbs 19:8
Matthew 22:37–39

Speak to Yourself

It's much better to talk to yourself than to listen to yourself. If we listen to negative thoughts, we can become defeated. Claim victory by speaking words of hope, strength and victory in Christ.

Nagging negative thoughts will always come your way. It's just one of the trials of life. However, you don't have to be defeated by suggestions such as 'You're useless', 'You're not good enough' or 'You can't do that.' These thoughts are not on your side and are designed to keep you suppressed. Fight back by refusing to allow them to germinate in your mind. Feel free to talk positively to yourself. These days, with everyone wired up to their earphones, talking to yourself is no longer seen as a sign of madness!

FOR FURTHER REFLECTION

1 Samuel 30:6

Create a Calming Atmosphere

*You can't control what happens on the outside,
but you can decide on a calming presence within.
Choose a calming response to any potentially
challenging situation.*

External factors that impact you such as a train strike, a leaky roof or a car engine failure are all examples of things that you cannot control. Getting angry, upset or frustrated will not solve the problem. Difficult though it may be, developing a quick turn-around in your response will go a long way towards establishing your calm. Accept the situation, and that you can't change it, but also accept that you can choose not to let the situation get to you.

FOR FURTHER REFLECTION

Isaiah 52:7
1 Peter 5:7

DAY 20

Be a Comforter

Being close to someone in their time of need is a powerful expression of showing friendship. You can't put a price on being there for a person in need.

You don't necessarily have to be a friend to someone to show comfort to them. Knowing a person you may be acquainted with who is going through a difficult time can be an opportunity to show support. Offering a listening ear, or just going out of your way to buy some necessary provisions, won't take you too far away from your daily routine. When a person is feeling low, any kind of support they receive becomes ingrained on their mind and will be remembered.

FOR FURTHER REFLECTION

2 Corinthians 1:3–4
John 14:16

DAY 21

Turn Your Water into Wine

*When things become routine and mundane,
it is time for a renewal. Christ can take the mundane
and transform it into something special through
a miracle of renewal.*

When Jesus turned water into wine at the wedding in Cana, he transformed something ordinary into something spectacular. If he did that with water, he can do that for each of our lives. The question is: do you want to continue in the routine and mundane or do you want to experience something special that will transform your understanding of God in a deeper way? Anything that enables you to have a bigger picture of God is something that it would definitely please God to arrange.

FOR FURTHER REFLECTION

John 2:1–11

Calm Your Mind

*Anxiety empowers and enlarges problems.
It blocks solutions. But answers flow more easily
and naturally from a peaceful state of mind.*

Never make permanent decisions based on temporary setbacks. When emotions are high we don't think too clearly and can make rash decisions. To safeguard against that, it's important that we develop a peaceful state of mind. Remove yourself from the troubling situation, take time to calm down and recollect your thoughts. Find a place that resonates calm within you and spend quality time there. Feel your body relax and your mind become clearer. Then, when you've steadied your nerves and feel your thoughts are clear, go back to the situation at hand and deal with it.

FOR FURTHER REFLECTION

Galatians 5:22
John 14:27

Reserve Judgement

*Before you condemn someone, remember where
God has brought you from. The Christian path is
a long and unseen one and everyone starts at
different points.*

We all have issues. Some are good at camouflaging theirs, while others are an open book. We all start the Christian path at different phases of life and at different start points. We all have different points of reference. Don't compare where you are to where someone else is along the path and think they are not doing as well as you. Just remember the mess you were in, in previous years and how God was merciful to you, then extend that favour to others who are still trying to find their way.

FOR FURTHER REFLECTION

1 Corinthians 6:11
Galatians 6:10

DAY 24

Know You're Not Alone

*Following Jesus does not exempt you from
life's storms. Remind yourself, however, who's with
you in the midst of the storm.*

We all pass through the storms of life. Being a Christian will not prevent you from experiencing them but your faith ought to help you face them rather than cowering away. It's in the midst of a storm, when things are dark and uncertain, that we find it most challenging. It's during these times we need to dig deep in our spiritual resolve and remember that even when we pass through the valley of death, we are to fear no evil for God is with us. The imagery of Christ being the 'Good Shepherd' with his staff is one that ought to give us comfort that he will guide us through.

FOR FURTHER REFLECTION

Psalm 23

DAY 25

Spread Kindness

It costs to be unkind, but pays to be kind.
No act of kindness, no matter how small,
is ever wasted.

It's the little acts of kindness that pay huge dividends. When you think of others, it lets them know they are special and thought of. There's too much misery and sadness in the world today and many people find it difficult to cope. When you spread kindness, it germinates seeds of hope and renewal for people who may otherwise feel life is a lost cause.

FOR FURTHER REFLECTION

Ecclesiastes 10:12

Keep Your Head

*Acting impulsively usually means things will
get worse before they get better, so don't panic.
Calm yourself and ask God for wisdom and help
even in the smallest and simplest things.*

Acting on the spur of the moment leads to unpredictable results. That may be OK with something that is rejuvenating, but may have the opposite effect if it involves a situation of panic or disarray. 'Think before you act' is always sound advice, but one step further is to take a moment to pray for wisdom. A prayer like that acknowledges you don't have the immediate solution and are depending on someone above and beyond you for help. A prayer for help will always reach the ears of God.

FOR FURTHER REFLECTION

2 Timothy 4:5

DAY 27

Keep Moving Forward!

Whenever you move forward, you will always have potential obstacles. Don't see them as stressful blocks to progress, but rather as stepping stones to success.

The ability to turn a negative situation into a positive one is a wonderful gift to have. Yet this gift is not reserved for the high and mighty – it can be yours too. It just takes a little determination not to allow an obstacle to impede your progress. Look beyond whatever is blocking you and refuse to let it hinder you. Sometimes obstacles are placed there to make you reflect on where you are presently, but if God has a plan for your life nothing can prevent it. So find a way to go under or around, or simply step over the obstacle and keep moving forward.

FOR FURTHER REFLECTION

2 Corinthians 4:15–17

Choose Self-control

*Your circumstances may be out of control,
but your character need not be. Choosing integrity
amidst adversity is a goal to be reached.*

It's easy to get carried away with the situation of the moment. When emotions run high, vision becomes impaired and the next thing you know, you're drawn into a situation that can easily compromise who you are and what you believe. Maintaining self-control is about not getting into a situation that brings out the worst in you. Knowing your weak points may help guard against exposure to them, but when you can maintain a spirit of calm, you rise above any potential mishap.

FOR FURTHER REFLECTION

2 Peter 1:5–6

Live an Honest Life

Your life resembles an iceberg. Only fifteen per cent is visible to others, while the remaining seventy-five per cent reveals your true identity. Make sure that there's no mismatch between you in public and private. Both elements should reveal your same true harmonious identity.

There's no better feeling than knowing there's consistency in who you are both in public and in private. Congruity is when there's harmony in how we behave across the board. When you live an honest life, you won't have to be constantly thinking about which version of you needs to be portrayed in any given situation.

FOR FURTHER REFLECTION

Micah 6:8

DAY 30

Step Out in Faith

Whenever you leave your comfort zone and step out in faith to follow God, you will be tested. However, you will still reach greater heights than if you settled for the status quo.

There's a part of us that likes to know what's coming next. It's all about being in control of our situation. There are times, however, when in order to see a greater work of God, we have to step out of that comfort zone. And when you do step out, it will challenge you to depend on God more to see you through the unknown. So trust God with your present situation – he won't let you fall when you take that leap of faith.

FOR FURTHER REFLECTION

2 Corinthians 4:15–17

Calm Down First

*Refuse to let negative emotions run amok
or dictate your response. Making permanent
decisions based on temporary feelings is dangerous.
Wait for the right moment to proceed.*

Spur-of-the-moment decisions are made on shaky ground. The intent may be right if you've been disappointed, hurt, shocked or angry, but the principle of that decision may not be well thought through. It's important to ensure all disappointment, hurt, shock and anger has dissipated. Let there be a time of calm reflection. Then after a while, tackle the issue at hand with a renewed mind.

FOR FURTHER REFLECTION

Psalm 37:5
Proverbs 3:5–6

DAY 32

Be Peaceable

'Blessed are the peacemakers' is a reference to those who can bring a calming influence to people who are in a stressful situation.

Becoming a mediator between two people can be rewarding. You become the 'go-between' that may be able to unite two lives together again. There may be times when the only person who can fill that role is you. So make yourself available and willing to step in to become a bridge, so that two people who may be at odds with each other can reach a point of understanding and forgiveness. You will have saved two souls from a life of misery.

FOR FURTHER REFLECTION

Romans 8:6
Mark 4:39
Matthew 5:9

DAY 33

Dispel Your Fears

Things are not as bad as you think – it's just the power of fear working on your mind as you face an unknown future. Disable that power through heartfelt prayer.

Fear can be crippling. It presents to the mind an unseen, frightening scenario that seldom, if ever, happens. But because you've pictured and internalised it in your mind, you then react accordingly. Dispel fear by taking the situation to God in prayer. The act of talking it out will go a long way, so invoke the power of God to banish the fearful imagery and replace it with a calm assurance that everything will be OK.

FOR FURTHER REFLECTION

Isaiah 41:10

Let God Guide You

When passing through uncharted territory,
team up with the one who sets you on steady
ground and makes your footing sure.

Following someone who knows exactly where they are going is reassuring. You don't want a situation of 'the blind leading the blind'. So stick with the expert who has trodden the path before you. Be comforted to know you won't get lost, because the Waymaker has a built-in satnav, compass, radar and every kind of navigation equipment to take you safely through to the other side.

FOR FURTHER REFLECTION

Proverbs 3:6
James 4:7–8
Isaiah 30:21

Breathe

*Slow abdominal breathing stimulates your
vagus nerve, which prompts relaxation in your nervous
system. It can actually bring down your stress levels.
Just stop what you're doing and give it a try.*

Controlled breathing in potential moments of nervousness or
panic is the aim. Usually the body, through its natural impulses,
reacts in a haphazard way in times of stress, causing physiological
responses such as sweating, palpitations and breathlessness. You
don't have to succumb to these occurrences. Just take deep, long
breaths and fill your lungs with air. Before long a fresh supply of
oxygen will reach your brain and trigger a new feeling of calm.

FOR FURTHER REFLECTION

Psalm 34:18

Accept God's View of You

*Remember you are a beautiful creation of God,
unique, wondrous and lovely. He made you amazing!
Don't let any mortal human being tell you otherwise.*

When someone gives you a compliment, how do you respond? Do you show appreciation and thank them? Or do you find yourself somewhat embarrassed and diminish the remarks with a counterstatement that undermines what was said? When you consider yourself to be a work of God's beautiful creativity, wonderfully made, then all compliments that come your way should be appreciated, accepted and believed. The bigger picture is that someone who gives you a compliment is really indirectly complimenting your Creator.

FOR FURTHER REFLECTION

Psalm 139:14

DAY 37

Tell Him Everything

Your problems are never too much for God.
Don't ever feel God's not interested in the minute
details of your life – you can't overwhelm him.

If God takes note of the sparrow in the sky and the flowers in the fields, then how much more does he take note of you! God notices everything. But he still wants you to tell him about them. The idea is that when you entrust him with your small issues they may not evolve to become bigger ones. So 'nip it in the bud' and as soon as something comes your way that's of slight concern, pass it on to the one who is able to absorb it. God would rather deal with the small issues than wait for you to find them big and wearisome.

FOR FURTHER REFLECTION

Matthew 6:25–34

DAY 38

Be Honest with God

*God already knows you inside out – you are
an open book to him. So enjoy an honest, sincere
relationship with God based on truth and openness.
Such a relationship only leads to a calm spirit.*

A relationship with God must be based on honesty. God is totally committed to us. He opens up to us by expressing his undying love and desire to be with us in all circumstances. The Bible is filled with the words of God, revealing his true identity to us. He wants us to reciprocate. You can be assured that when we open up to him, it's in full confidence and what we share is not going anywhere else. So tell him the truth – God may be the only one who you can tell.

FOR FURTHER REFLECTION

Psalm 139:13–16

DAY 39

Get in Tune

So often we're just trying to get through the day and we're not in tune with the nuances of what we're doing. Don't be caught up in that trap – be in tune with life's lessons for your soul.

Sometimes we can find ourselves just going through the motions. The routines of life become mundane and before you know it you're on autopilot. The next thing you know, the week has blown past. It's in these seemingly everyday tasks that we can switch off and not really focus on the situation at hand. Yet even in our everyday routines there are important life lessons that need to be learned, so stay focused and watch out for things that seem minor but can have major effects.

FOR FURTHER REFLECTION

Colossians 3:2
Matthew 6:33

Get Up Again

*Don't beat yourself up when you fall or let God down.
We are all susceptible to sin and temptation, but we
serve a merciful Father who is infinitely patient
with our spiritual growth.*

The art of being a Christian is simply not staying down when you fall. There is an infinite supply of God's mercy, but we need to acknowledge it and not feel God has run out of patience. You may feel you've tried too many times and still can't get this Christian life right – if that's the case, welcome to the countless many others who have felt the same way, but have still stuck in there. So get up again, brush yourself down and keep going!

FOR FURTHER REFLECTION

Proverbs 24:16

Be Specific

When talking to God tell him exactly how you feel, rather than saying 'I'm angry' or 'I'm sad.' You have a plethora of distinctions and complexities that can fine-tune what you're experiencing.

If you can express exactly how you feel, it goes a long way towards helping get stuff off your chest. Being specific fine-tunes your actual feelings, rather than just using broad terms to express what you're going through. It may take a bit of time to process your emotions. Ask yourself the question 'Why am I feeling the way I'm feeling?', then answer your own question.

FOR FURTHER REFLECTION

Ephesians 4:25
Proverbs 11:3
Proverbs 12:22

DAY 42

Check Your Attitude

*Nothing will hinder you in life as severely as
a bad attitude. Ask God to show you if the attitude
you have now is Christ-like or not. If it isn't,
let it go before it destroys you.*

When we are in conflict with someone, our usual tendency is to defend our own emotional responses and blame the other person for not being reasonable. It takes maturity of character to first check on your own response to, and feelings about, the situation and to see if your attitude needs to be adjusted. This is sometimes difficult to do because we tend to justify our behaviours. Step outside of the situation, reflect on your approach and see if any of the conflict is actually a result of your own behaviour.

FOR FURTHER REFLECTION

Ephesians 4:31

Reject Negative Thoughts

*As soon as the enemy sends negative thoughts
to your mind, stop them by determining that you will
not agree, and don't listen to his voice any more.*

In the course of a day so many voices vie for your attention. Most of these voices are not audible and seek entrance to our thoughts. Sometimes they are placed in our minds by Satan, who seeks to discredit us for striving to be a Christian. Negative thoughts need to be identified and captured. It's in the entry phase that they need to be addressed. If left, they will assimilate into our subconscious and influence our behaviour. Don't let this happen!

FOR FURTHER REFLECTION

1 Peter 5:8–9

Choose the Right Outlook

*Misery is only an option. You can always choose to
be unhappy and pessimistic, but you can also choose
to be happy and optimistic.*

Your outlook in life really depends on your 'in-look' at life. If you can see potential positives in every negative situation or can turn disappointments into appointments for growth then you can bypass living a life of misery. It's not easy when going through depressing times. Everything seems bleak and dark. However, in those periods remember that we all go through low moments but that's exactly what they are – moments. Believe that it's momentary and a better situation is just around the corner!

FOR FURTHER REFLECTION

Psalm 1:1–3
Psalm 97:12

Be Real

There's no need to put on a performance with God.
Just be real and know he totally understands everything
about you and what you go through in life.

Authenticity is the way forward with God and with everyone else. That's not to mean you have to share everything about yourself with everyone, but it does mean what you choose to share is genuine. Living a lie is so much harder because you have to constantly remember what your last lie was to continue the pattern of deception. That's a lot to keep up with! So choose the best and simpler option – choose today to start living a genuine, honest, real life and watch all the pressure of keeping up a facade fade away!

FOR FURTHER REFLECTION

John 8:32

Thank God for Unexpected Blessings

*Sometimes God's blessings come through
unexpected circumstances. Look out for them
in every situation in life.*

We can have the tendency when referring to blessings to think of the big, nice things that happen to us. When we embark on that path we miss out on the many small and seemingly insignificant blessings along life's way each day. Watch how children point out interesting and little things when you take them out for a walk. Now apply the same practice yourself!

FOR FURTHER REFLECTION

Deuteronomy 1:11
Philippians 4:19

Stay Hopeful

Your trials are temporary – they won't last for ever.
Stay positive. If God brought them to you,
he will bring you through them.

The trials of life are tough. No one likes going through them, but it's the reality of life. We all go through testing times. These trials, however, almost always serve some kind of purpose. If you're experiencing a hard time, it may be happening for a reason which you can't see right now, but will ultimately help in your personal growth and development.

FOR FURTHER REFLECTION

Hebrews 10:23
2 Corinthians 4:18

Wait for Change

The seasons of life are exactly that – seasons.
When you find yourself in the 'winter of discontent',
hold on – it will pass. The spring of new beginnings
is just around the corner.

The cycle of life can be likened to the seasons of the year. We all like the summer where things are bright and glorious, but the autumn and winter seasons can also be a period of potential blossoming and growth. So during the cold, dark nights of winter, don't despair. Soon you will see the daffodils and tulips of personal growth. No season lasts for ever, so just wait for the change.

FOR FURTHER REFLECTION

Romans 12:12
Psalm 40:1

Follow God's Blueprint for Life

An unfulfilled life is one without purpose –
with Christ, you not only get a purpose, but a plan
to go with it.

God has a unique plan, tailor-made and especially designed for you. No one else is suited for that plan. First, you were created to know and honour your Creator, then to be led into living out God's purpose and plan for your life! The whole journey of life is to discover that purpose.

FOR FURTHER REFLECTION

Jeremiah 29:11

DAY 50

Claim Your Joy

Today God's word for you is: 'weeping may endure for a night, but joy comes in the morning'. Don't lose hope – God's already on your case!

God works behind the scenes in our lives. We can't see him in action but be assured he's working on your case. It's in the darkest hour, when we feel there is no hope and we believe God has forgotten about us, that we often feel the lowest. But as the sun rises in the morning, so does the confidence that your darkest hour was just a turning point. The morning light of joy and radiance will dispel the gloom and tears that filled your heart during the night.

FOR FURTHER REFLECTION

Psalm 30:5
Nehemiah 8:10

DAY 51

Stretch Your Faith

Miracles don't just happen – it takes an act of faith.
Stretch your faith in God a little further and
see what God will do for you.

It seems easier to have faith in the bus driver, the airline pilot or the taxi driver when our life is in their hands. Yet somehow when it comes to having faith in God we struggle. Think of God as the one who holds the entire universe in his hands and who has put everything in place so that the starry heavens above move in unison. Remember, he is the God who created man out of nothing, breathed life into his nostrils and declares 'There's nothing too hard for me', so stretch your faith and let him perform a miracle in your life!

FOR FURTHER REFLECTION

Matthew 9:9

Expect Great Things

*God has great things in store for you today:
expect them, look for them and believe them!*

Any loving parent simply wants to shower their children with good things. Love, affection and a secure home are all basic necessities provided by loving parents. The child does not expect any of these things, but receives them simply because of who they are. Likewise, God our heavenly Father seeks to shower us with good things. It's not even because we deserve it, but it's because of who we are. His unconditional love for us, his children, means that we will always be the recipients of great things.

FOR FURTHER REFLECTION

Isaiah 55:9

DAY 53

Keep Your Hopes Up

Life can become wearisome, but instead of going around complaining, put a smile on your face – your attitude impacts your altitude.

Your position in life does not have to dictate your disposition. You may have been handed a disadvantage in some way, but you don't have to let that affect your outlook on life. Most of the happiest people in the world are those who have little or nothing, but yet make the best out of what they have. Rather than look at what you don't have, appreciate and treasure what you do have. This inner satisfaction and joy can't help but break through on your countenance.

FOR FURTHER REFLECTION

Philippians 4:1

DAY 54

Take That Step

Taking a new step is often what we fear the most, yet our real fear ought to be standing still and doing nothing. Trust God with each new step you take in your life.

Watching a child learn to walk is an amazing life lesson, as is teaching a child to ride a bike. In both situations, they will fall multiple times. The child may have a little cry, but before long they are trying again. Isn't life's journey like that? When we try something new we may fall and have a little cry, but what makes a person successful is that they get back up and try again.

FOR FURTHER REFLECTION

Joshua 1:7–9

Spend Time Wisely

We all get 24 hours, 1,440 minutes, 86,400 seconds each day. See today's allocation as a gift of life to do something meaningful for yourself and for others.

Maximising your time doesn't mean trying to cram in everything to meet your deadline. What's important is having a quality of time that's meaningful to you and those around you. Special moments can be brief, but become memorable because of who they are shared with or what you enjoyed if you spent those moments alone. So don't rush through your day thinking 'When my work is all done, then I can relax' – maximise your time by appreciating life's lessons along the way.

FOR FURTHER REFLECTION

Psalm 90:12

Live for Today

Worry doesn't rid tomorrow of its challenges, but it robs today of its joy. Remember, God gives you today's strength for today's needs.

Today is a new day. That means a new supply of energy, strength and hope. This gift of life and all that comes with it is not meant to be spent dealing with issues we can't control in the future; it is meant to be spent dealing with what's in hand today. Worry depletes the body of vital nutrients needed to get through today. Do yourself a favour and guard your mental and emotional reserves. You need to be on top form today!

FOR FURTHER REFLECTION

1 Peter 5:7

Be Assured

*God uses the good, the bad and the ugly experiences
of your life to prepare you for your next challenge.
Everything works together for good!*

Nothing is wasted. Everything you have been through in
your life can be used as collateral to face your todays and your
tomorrows. Your past may contain some unsightly experiences
but they were what made you who you are today. Nothing
is thrown away – everything we have done in the past is good
fertiliser for cultivating a better future!

FOR FURTHER REFLECTION

Romans 8:28

Follow God's Way

God wants us to be happy and joyful.
When we live a life according to God's will
we will be happy and joyful.

If God created us and made us who we are, then surely he has the blueprints for what makes us enjoy life. Being designed by God also comes with a list of life's instructions. If we follow the instructions and guidelines which are found in the Bible, then we will function at our optimum level and the best will be brought out of us.

FOR FURTHER REFLECTION

Deuteronomy 30:19

God's Got Your Back

Whatever you may face today, remember
that God is greater than your greatest opposition,
so go through your day full of confidence
that he will work it out.

You are not alone. Unseen to human eyes is one who watches over us in all our daily endeavours. One of Jesus' last words were: 'Lo, I am with you always, even to the end of the age.' These words declare his unfailing love towards us. With that in mind we can be assured that God is just a prayer away. When you call on him his response will be: 'I am here.' With that assurance, go forward in confidence knowing you have a mighty force with you!

FOR FURTHER REFLECTION

Romans 8:31
Matthew 28:20

Give God the Credit

*God loves to start with nothing. So when he
provides a way for you, there is no doubt who has
the power and who ought to get the credit.*

If you think not much can be achieved through you, then maybe that's a quality God is looking for. Feelings of inadequacy or unpreparedness lead you to see your own insufficiency. That's where God takes over. He takes your weaknesses and uses you to accomplish things you thought you never could achieve with your own strength. All you can do then is say 'It wasn't me that did that, but God!'

FOR FURTHER REFLECTION

John 15:5

Take Another Look

It's easy to ask 'Why me?' when going through difficult times; but it takes spiritual depth to consider asking 'Why not me?' Every trial serves a unique purpose.

The question 'Why me?' is born from frustration and a lack of understanding of the situation we are facing. Flipping the situation around and seeing that your plight has been brought on for some reason or purpose takes a lot of faith. Asking 'Why not me?' takes it a step further. But when you think of people who are much worse off than you, it ought to be a question we all should consider!

FOR FURTHER REFLECTION

Romans 8:18
Job 13:15

Let God Take Control

Stop trying so hard to make things happen on your terms and allow God to make things happen for you on his terms.

When you commit your way to the Lord, you have to be prepared to let him lead. Trying to force open new doors in life, then asking God to bless you, is a futile approach. Let God lead. He knows the best route for you to take and how to avoid the pitfalls and dead ends. Wouldn't you rather have a mountaineer to guide you up a mountain you've never climbed? Then let God be God!

FOR FURTHER REFLECTION

Proverbs 3:5–6

DAY 63

Reach Your Potential

Jesus knows the worst about you, yet still believes the best in you. He sees your potential – what you can become through him.

We all long for someone to believe in us. You may have fallen short of your true potential because someone put you down when you were younger. Someone told you you couldn't do something or damaged your self-esteem. You don't have to stay wounded. God knows how to validate you. He sees what you can't see, but what he sees is a possibility, a promise and a great big bundle of potential.

FOR FURTHER REFLECTION

1 Samuel 16:7

Claim Your Victory Today

*You don't have to wait until the trial is over
before thanking God for getting you through.
Thank him throughout the process and
claim the victory in advance.*

If you can reach out to God with an attitude of thankfulness while still going through your challenge, then you have learned a spiritually mature way of doing things. Don't wait until it's all over to express your appreciation to God for getting you through. Do so now in confidence that a positive outcome is already guaranteed.

FOR FURTHER REFLECTION

Romans 8:31–32
Galatians 5:1

Avoid Personal Recognition

*If you're asking God to make you bigger
instead of better, you may be disappointed.
God's priority is spiritual growth.*

Thinking of great things for yourself? While it's good to think big, what is your motive? Trying to achieve things to boost your ego or status among your peers is drawing attention to yourself and all there is about you. God can help you progress and grow in life, but it starts from the inside first. When God is allowed to develop the character within, your standing in life will naturally be enlarged.

FOR FURTHER REFLECTION

Luke 16:10

Be Patient with Yourself

Remember you're still a work in progress –
God's not finished with you yet.

The work of growth takes a lifetime. It's a course you never graduate from. That's why you need to be patient with yourself and others around you who are also in a process of growth. From a spiritual standpoint, the closer you get to God, the more you begin to see your true self. Further details of your character are uncovered and the layers of your life slowly reveal the core of who you really are. As long as the trajectory of your life is in the right direction, then let the work of fine-tuning your life be left with God.

FOR FURTHER REFLECTION

Jeremiah 18:4

Cast Your Burdens on Him

Stress is a normal part of life.
Our ability to avoid it may be limited, but
managing stress is possible when you cast
all your cares upon God.

Whatever becomes a concern to you becomes a concern to God. He has a personal interest in your life and all that perplexes you. Knowing someone is generally interested in you makes it easier to be willing to share and open up to that person. God makes himself available, but wants you to not only share your concerns, but to entrust him with them. Offloading is exactly that, you take the load off yourself and transfer it onto God.

FOR FURTHER REFLECTION

Matthew 11:28–29

Forgive Yourself

If God is willing to forgive and forget your past sins, mistakes and wrong choices, then it's time for you to stop beating yourself up with guilt and shame, receive his mercy and move on.

We may think we hold no malice or hatred towards anyone and that forgiveness is not an issue we struggle with, but there may be someone we have unconsciously failed to forgive. That person may be yourself! Are there people you may have hurt in the past who you feel guilty about? If so, then you have become the victim. No amount of beating yourself up can solve the problem. If God is willing to forgive you, then make steps to forgive yourself!

FOR FURTHER REFLECTION

Philippians 3:13

Stay Faithful During Adversity

*There are things we learn about God and ourselves
that can only occur through times of adversity.
Trust him through the process – it serves a
higher purpose.*

The storms of life often rip through our lives leaving us exposed and wounded. They can also strip away at the personal protective barriers that reveal our true inner selves. We begin to see ourselves reacting to a situation we have never encountered before, revealing something new about ourselves that was hitherto untapped, such as greater inner strength, higher tolerance or tougher resilience. Consider this a blessing in disguise, for it also enables us to approach God in a way we have never done before.

FOR FURTHER REFLECTION

Psalm 34:18

Stand on His Promises

*Life is much more calming when you decide
to stand on God's Word and trust him regardless
of the circumstances.*

Having faith involves the ability to move forward positively. Faith demands behaving in accordance with what you believe will happen before you see it happen. When your faith is founded on a belief in God's promises, your whole disposition will change. You will accept God's promise of help in time of trouble, or to get you through difficult times, and as a result you will no longer stress yourself over the situation. You will begin to act in complete trust that God will take care of things for you, leaving you in a state of calm composure.

FOR FURTHER REFLECTION

Proverbs 3:7

Stay Blessed

*What's amazing about grace? It's the fact
that you are alive right now and God's keeping your
heart beating each day.*

Life is a precious gift, never to be taken for granted. The moment we awake, there's another opportunity to recognise that we are blessed. So celebrate each new day with a fresh supply of appreciation and zeal. It's a new opportunity to make a difference to somebody else, and to yourself. No matter how dark and dreary it may look outside, the desire to make a difference lies within.

FOR FURTHER REFLECTION

Numbers 6:24–26

Rest in His Arms

We can call our heavenly Father 'Abba', meaning
'Daddy'. How wonderful that God wants us to crawl
into his lap, feel secure in his arms, rest our heads
on his chest and call him 'Daddy'.

One of the sweetest sights is seeing a newborn baby fast asleep in its mother's arms. It's a picture of complete calm and total trust. That's exactly how our heavenly Father wants us to approach him. First, he wants us to see him not as someone high and lofty, or with grand titles, but simply as our daddy. Second, he wants you to feel comfortable enough to picture yourself lying down and resting in his loving arms. Capture the picture of that sleeping baby – now imagine yourself doing the same thing in your heavenly daddy's arms.

FOR FURTHER REFLECTION

Romans 8:15

Be Content

Happiness is not about getting what you want –
it's about enjoying what you've got. So keep your
perspective and be grateful every day.

The last of the ten commandments talks about not coveting our neighbours' goods. It's a practical commandment because it teaches us to be accepting of what we do have. When we can learn to be content with our present situation, we begin to find more reasons to be thankful. While people equate material possessions with happiness, it's important to see through that facade and recognise that happiness comes when we make use of what we do have, without always yearning for an upgrade or a replacement or the latest version.

FOR FURTHER REFLECTION

1 Timothy 6:8

Be Still and Know

Following Jesus can't be done at a sprint – you can't run ahead of the one who's leading. So slow down, pace yourself and enjoy the day-by-day journey with Jesus.

Sometimes in our zeal to follow God we want to learn too much too quickly. The disciple Peter thought he was ready to stand up for Christ, but that same day denied him three times. He thought he was standing firm, but he was still on shaky ground. Spiritual growth takes time, so don't get upset with yourself if you find you're still struggling in a certain area. Change will come, as long as you stay in there and keep learning. In the meantime, enjoy the everyday journey of new spiritual discoveries.

FOR FURTHER REFLECTION

Matthew 6:34
Matthew 6:11

Be Comforted

One of the roles of the Holy Spirit is that of comforter – it means 'to be called to the side of'. That's exactly what we receive when we wrestle with our everyday issues of life.

You thought you wouldn't make it, but you did. You thought you couldn't overcome, but you have. When you look back, you will realise you've been through some really challenging times. What's not so noticeable is who's been with you through it all. When you looked back during those times and saw only one set of footprints in the sand, they were not yours. It was in those darkest hours that you were carried. God comforts us in our darkest times by actually drawing near and being by our side!

FOR FURTHER REFLECTION

2 Corinthians 1:3–4

Live Meaningfully

Your greatest gift is your God-given life.
Only you can decide how to make the best of it.

Life is a gift. All gifts need to be nurtured and looked after and they will stay around for a long time. You are the steward of your life. You decide how your life will play out. You may not have started with the same privileges or fortunes as others, but in reality those things rarely help to make life easy. Your quality of life is not determined by the luxuries and lavish lifestyle that money can buy. It's determined by appreciating the special people around you, who are there to enhance your life, and resolving to make the best of the opportunities that come your way.

FOR FURTHER REFLECTION

Ecclesiastes 9:10

Seek God's Providence

In times of uncertainty, be reminded that God has already sorted out your circumstances in ways that you cannot yet see.

God loves to work behind the scenes. That way he keeps you on your toes as you learn to depend on him. If he reveals his hand too soon, the timing will not be right and you may not appreciate a premature outcome. The timing has to be perfect, and in our impatience we have to learn to wait on God. He is always on time and when his solution is ready he will reveal it to you, and then you will understand why you had to go through what you went though. It's all about timing!

FOR FURTHER REFLECTION

Jeremiah 33:3

Create Your Joy

Pure joy may be found in the most unlikely places –
with laughing children, relaxing on your wonky old
sofa or beside a warm fireside on a cold day.
Joy is where you find it.

Those who are happiest most often are those who recognise that joy comes in the simplest of things. Those opportunities are not based on material possessions, status or educational attainment. Money can't buy happiness – that we already know – so we find it in our approach to life. Joy comes to anybody rich or poor, who sees the value in their lives and accounts themselves as blessed. The good thing is that God is not partial – he gives us all opportunities in which to find and create our own joy.

FOR FURTHER REFLECTION

John 10:10

Look for His Enablings

No other day is like today – it brings its unique share of blessings. They're all around, you just have to notice them.

No two days are the same. You may have had a bad day yesterday, but that doesn't mean the same will happen today. That's the beauty of a new day. It's always different and provides new opportunities to build on yesterday and learn something new. If yesterday was a good day, today could be even better! So embrace this new 24-hour period of life and be thankful in advance for what will happen.

FOR FURTHER REFLECTION

Deuteronomy 28:1–13

Express Your Love

*If you constantly love someone, constantly tell them.
No amount of gifts can replace the deep-seated
security of being told you are loved.*

Taking people for granted is our greatest omission. Too often our best speeches about a loved one are made at their funeral and the most beautiful displays of flowers are laid around the burial place. Get your priorities right and stop holding back on expressing your feelings! Trust me, it won't hurt if you look someone in the eyes, express how special they are to you and tell them that you love them. Do it while they can see and hear you. Do it often because time is short and do it now before the opportunity is missed!

FOR FURTHER REFLECTION

Song of Solomon 8:7

DAY 81

Value Loved Ones

The sweetest things in life are those you cannot buy – the gift of good health, the loyalty of friends, a supportive family. Don't take any of these for granted.

It's only fair that the best things in life are free. If a price were placed on happiness, it would be outsourced to the richest five per cent of the world. So the onus is on us to recognise the source of happiness. It's not rocket science – it's simply found first in loving God with all our heart, soul and mind and strength, and then extending that to the people God places in our lives. Love is the basis of all true friendships, and when we recognise who those special ones are, we can learn to express that love in many and various ways.

FOR FURTHER REFLECTION

Luke 10:27

Appreciate the Little Things

*The best things come in small packages – a word
of cheer, a warm hug, a card with meaningful words,
a bunch of flowers. Sometimes the smallest
things speak the loudest.*

Little things are only little in size, not in their effects. They may be called little because they seem insignificant or easy to obtain – this makes them all the better because then they are available to all. So a little word of hope, a little word of encouragement or a little token or gift speaks loud volumes. Don't overthink what to do for someone in case they feel overwhelmed. Check your motive – big gifts demand a bigger acknowledgement to the giver and it ought not be about you! So be simple, be genuine and let the little acts of love speak for themselves!

FOR FURTHER REFLECTION

Luke 19:17

Don't Neglect Yourself

Be your own best friend, reverse the golden rule –
the kindness you do to others, do also to yourself.

The reverse side of always being there for other people is that you yourself can become neglected. It may be that you are self-less in what you do, which is indeed honourable. However, when you do things for others without caring for yourself, you soon find your well of gratitude and love begins to run dry. You have to replenish your own well so that you can be better positioned to reach out to others. So give yourself some kindness. Show yourself some love. Whatever you do to others, apply some of it to yourself. You deserve it!

FOR FURTHER REFLECTION

Galatians 5:14

Embrace Your Uniqueness

You are unique – there are things only you can do.
So appreciate the gifts God has given you.

You have a gift which belongs only to you. You can administer that gift in your own style, through your own personality with your own approach – that's what makes it unique. Others may have similar gifts, but it's about how you use yours. Your gift may yet to be discovered, so ask God to reveal it to you. It may be that you're just naturally good at something, or you enjoy doing a particular task. These are all gifts that come from who you are. Enjoy and develop them. They are what defines your contribution to the world.

FOR FURTHER REFLECTION

2 Timothy 1:6

Have a Merry Heart

*Laughter lowers the blood pressure, keeps illness
at bay, reduces worry, tones up your nervous system
and makes your face more pleasant to look at!
That ought to be sufficient reason to laugh.*

It's amazing what laughter can do. First, it's contagious – you're bound to laugh out loud when in the presence of someone who does. It also actually relaxes your face as you're using fewer muscles. There are several health benefits, but most of all, it just gives you that feel-good factor. So why do we laugh less the older we get? Whatever the reasons, as long as you have lungs and a mouth, don't let anything stop you from having a good, belly-deep, laugh-out-loud time!

FOR FURTHER REFLECTION

Proverbs 17:22

Spread Love

*The most valuable gifts are priceless – compliments,
encouragement and a listening ear.*

It doesn't take much to be an instrument of love. It's not about
the lavish gifts which are here today and gone tomorrow. It is,
however, about the little things that can make a lasting impression.
An encouraging word fitly spoken at the right time, the
warmth of an assuring hug, or just giving someone your undivided
attention while they share the burdens on their heart – love is
all about making yourself available for these special moments in
someone's life that will be treasured for ever.

FOR FURTHER REFLECTION

1 Thessalonians 5:11

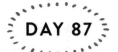

DAY 87

Have a Good Cry

The end product of shedding a tear or two is a feeling of calm. Expressing pent-up emotions through tears releases tension and produces a state of well-being.

Tears consist of water, salt and several different proteins. However, putting these elements aside, tears also provide a release for more weighty things – the pressures of life, the deepest disappointments that overwhelm us, the sadness that comes through grief and many other emotional feelings we experience. Tears are the body's release of the heaviest burdens and the avenue for the greatest feeling of calm afterwards. If you must cry, don't bottle it up, let the tears flow and let the healing begin. It's OK to cry!

FOR FURTHER REFLECTION

Lamentations 3:22–23

Retreat to Advance

*Remember, silence is golden and solitude is essential
for mental, emotional, physical and spiritual renewal.
We should all find time for a moment to be
by ourselves.*

If it was necessary for Jesus, then it surely must be necessary for us. Jesus made it his duty to find quiet places. There he would get away from the busyness of life and be alone with his father. Christ set the perfect example, showing us how we can be recharged just by getting away from the many things that distract us. Don't be stifled by life's demands: find your quiet place – a place where you can truly be alone with God without interruptions.

FOR FURTHER REFLECTION

Matthew 6:6

DAY 89

See the Bigger Picture

Disappointments will always happen in life.
Rather than seeing them as setbacks, see them as
the restraining arm of God, shielding you from
a worse fate.

We will never know how the protection of God covers us each day. When we go through challenging times, we may cry out to God for help and feel that our burden is too much to bear. It's in times like these that we must also look at the bigger picture. You're here today because you have been protected by the unfailing hand of God, guiding you in dangerous situations so you can come through unscathed.

FOR FURTHER REFLECTION

Psalm 34:7

DAY 90

Recharge

The accumulation of problems can sap your energy and deplete you. Take time to replenish and recharge by renewing your mind with the many promises of God in his Word.

Each new day brings a fresh supply of potential issues and problems. If we're living in the real world with work, relationships, children and bills, we will always be exposed to challenging situations. That's why it's important to guard yourself from emotional and mental fatigue and burnout. Replace the vital life nutrients that can often be depleted by nurturing your mind on things which can renew and reinforce your inner strength. The Bible contains countless promises of strength, hope and endurance. Feed on them!

FOR FURTHER REFLECTION

Isaiah 40:31

Remember the Golden Rule

We tend to hurt the ones we love the most.
This is a paradox that needs to stop, for in hurting
your loved one you ultimately hurt yourself.

Why do we do that? Hurt the ones we love the most? OK, so we may not do it intentionally and probably feel awful afterwards, but some damage is done. It's so much harder trying make up for a wrong act towards someone than just learning to think before we act or respond. Thinking about how you would like to be treated in a given situation allows you to take stock of how you respond to the other person. It doesn't take much to process that. Just think first, and ask yourself: 'How would I like to be treated?'

FOR FURTHER REFLECTION

1 John 3:15
Matthew 7:12

Become an Instrument of Love

*Becoming a channel of God's love is the best
way to express love. All you need to do is ask God to
demonstrate love to someone else through you.*

Human love can often fall short. It's conditional – show love to me and I'll reciprocate. Our love is partial – I will show greater love to those who believe the same things as I do, or who look more like me. Human love is also limited – it goes up to a certain point, but not beyond! God's love is unconditional, impartial and unlimited. Let his love flow through you to others!

FOR FURTHER REFLECTION

Matthew 5:46
Psalm 63:3

Treat Yourself Well

To give your best you must feel your best.
To feel your best you must look after yourself
and treat yourself well.

There's only one version of you. No one else is like you. You're unique in so many ways. So because you are one of a kind, make sure you treat yourself with special care. There's nothing wrong in treating yourself from time to time and putting yourself first! When you do that, your body will speak back through an inner glow of joy that says: 'Thank you for making me special today and allowing me feel I'm worth it!'

FOR FURTHER REFLECTION

Micah 6:8

DAY 94

Spread Love

*Once in a while we all need to hear the words:
'I think you're wonderful.' Start the ball rolling and
express that to someone, then see how quickly
those words are returned to you.*

Too often we hold back on expressing words of affirmation and admiration for someone. We tend to be quick to criticise and express our negativity when someone makes a mistake, but we must find a balance. When you affirm someone by saying that their hair looks good, expressing gratitude for something they've done or heaping praise on them for something they've achieved, you can guarantee that you are sowing seeds of confidence, self-belief and assurance in someone's life.

FOR FURTHER REFLECTION

Songs of Songs 8:7

Thank God for Who You Are

*God's love to you is unique. It's as if you were
the only person in the universe.*

Yes, there may be around 7.7 billion people in the world today, but God sees you as a singular entity. He sees you as though you were the only one. Not only that, but his love is showered upon you without measure. God's love is not something that has to be shared around and reaches a certain quota. God's love for you belongs to you, and God's love for me belongs to me. That's the beauty of an omniscient God – he is able to treat everyone as a unique, special person.

FOR FURTHER REFLECTION

Jeremiah 31:3

Take It to the Lord

The inspired hymn writer Joseph Scriven wrote:
'O what peace we often forfeit, O what needless pain
we bear, all because we do not carry everything
to God in prayer!' How true!

Sometimes we can be our own worst enemies. We put ourselves into difficult situations for no reason other than our own misjudgements or poor decisions. As a result we go through needless agony and heartache. Trying to dig our way out is not the best solution. It's simply acknowledging that there is someone much bigger than you or me who knows how to deal with all problems. So next time you find yourself in a difficulty, remember to release it to God.

FOR FURTHER REFLECTION

Philippians 4:6–7

DAY 97

Develop a Big Heart

When your heart rather than your purse becomes the reservoir of your giving, you will find it full at all times.

Giving is usually associated with giving money to someone to help them on their way. While this may be helpful for temporary needs, there will always be a shortfall. Money can't fill the void that we all have that needs to be filled by someone above and beyond us. That's why so many millionaires find themselves still unfulfilled. Reaching out with genuine heartfelt love to someone in need doesn't come with a price tag. It leaves a valuable investment that far outweighs any monetary deposit.

FOR FURTHER REFLECTION

Malachi 3:10

DAY 98

Identify Your Loved Ones

Part of ageing healthily is taking time to develop and nurture the social relationships you have.

People feel happy when they are around the special people in their lives. Too often we allow the busyness of life to rob us of quality time with those who are important to us. Prioritise your time. Identify those in your life who are precious and make an effort to value and enhance those special relationships.

FOR FURTHER REFLECTION

Proverbs 27:17

Believe in Yourself

*Take time today to dwell on the amazing thought
that you are absolutely precious in the sight of God.
You are truly loved, valued, special and one of a kind.*

You are indeed special in the eyes of God. When you really begin to believe that, it will transform how you view yourself. Reading words of affirmations about how you are esteemed in the eyes of God will only reinforce God's truth. Inwardly the process of belief in God's estimation of you will impact your thoughts, which in turn will be displayed in your behaviour.

FOR FURTHER REFLECTION

Psalm 17:8

Keep Fit

*When we engage in simple exercise it creates
a feeling of well-being produced by endorphins
released from the brain. Start your day stretching,
walking, jogging or cycling to get the blood
whizzing through the arteries.*

Exercise is not always a 'get-up-and-go' thing for many people. It takes effort, planning and sacrifice. However, when you can overcome the obstacles and take some form of exercise, the payoff is rewarding. You feel you've achieved something worthwhile – it's invigorating and you feel a sense of accomplishment. That's the work of the endorphins, rewarding you with a wonderful feel-good factor. Next time you have to get out of bed to exercise, just think of the rewards that will come after!

FOR FURTHER REFLECTION

3 John 2

Worship Him

Worship is an exhilarating experience.
The focus is not on you – in that moment you are
acknowledging the one who deserves your attention.
So get over your inhibitions, look heavenwards,
lift up your hands and worship God.

Worship can be expressed in many ways according to your personality or culture. The main thing is that God becomes the centre of attention. He knows your heart and the feelings that are directed toward him. Picture football fans in the stadium singing, cheering and chanting the names of their players as their team closes in on a win. It's an ecstatic atmosphere – it's also worship, but directed towards their team. If football fans can allow the euphoria of joy to overwhelm them, then surely we can in response to all that God has done for us!

FOR FURTHER REFLECTION

Psalm 134:2
Psalm 29:2

Move Forward on Your Knees

When life brings you to your knees, stay there and exercise the power of prayer. Soon you will be back on your feet, only this time more empowered and ready to face the world!

There are times when in order to move forward and overcome certain hindrances or problems you have to get down to some serious prayer! Pouring your heart out to God to help you tackle a difficulty or a heartfelt prayer for your wayward child, are prayers that come deep from within. On your knees, prostrate before God, bow down before him and humble yourself in his presence.

FOR FURTHER REFLECTION

Matthew 21:22

Pace Yourself

*Pushing yourself may take the next item off
your to-do list, but at what price? Do yourself
a favour and listen to your body!*

When you become determined at all costs to finish your to-do list or meet certain deadlines in one day, there's always a negative payback waiting for you. You might not notice it straight away, but when compulsive behaviour dictates how you govern your day someone will be worse off. It may be you or those around you. Pace yourself! Focus on what's urgent and important first, then set yourself a cut-off time to stop. Tomorrow is another day!

FOR FURTHER REFLECTION

Psalm 46:10

Be Inspired by Water

Watching a flowing river, a babbling brook,
a tranquil lake or the vast open sea are all therapeutic
to the soul. Such scenes will inspire you with
calm and awe.

The simple things in nature are often the most powerful for calming the soul. We often don't notice them as we rush through our day. When you can pay attention to the flow of nature it does something special inside. Make an effort to look out for those hidden acts of nature speaking out to you, saying: 'Slow down, stop for a while and please observe me.'

FOR FURTHER REFLECTION

Psalm 137:1

Stay Calm

*Calmness is the ability to develop and maintain a
state of inner assurance and tranquillity when things
around you are chaotic and upside down.*

There are days when your problems and concerns may feel so large and so looming you just can't escape them. Questions about the future will fill your mind: 'What if things don't get better? What if the worst happens?' The weight is enough to sink you. Remember your problems will never outmatch God's power. With every problem you face he will meet you where you are and lift you up. Just look up!

FOR FURTHER REFLECTION

John 14:27

Face Your Day Triumphantly

Faced with a challenging task today?
Remember you 'can do all things through Christ
who strengthens you'.

Sometimes you're stuck in a dark, emotional place in life, but you can't put your finger on why. You can start to trace the feeling back to its source by having more self-awareness. So often we're just trying to get through today and we're not exactly in tune with the nuances of what we're doing. Whatever is going on *in us* eventually comes *out of us*. Once we acknowledge our behaviour, we can begin to identify what feelings or needs are part of it. So take an inventory. What have you been doing lately?

FOR FURTHER REFLECTION

Philippians 4:13

Heed the Warnings

Headaches, migraines, exhaustion and stress
are warning signs from the body that the pendulum
of calm has swung too far in the wrong direction.
Do yourself a favour and let your body heal.

Your body is your best teacher. If you listen to the promptings of your body you will hear instruction and guidance on how to proceed with your life. When we ignore the calls of our body to rest, sleep, eat or rise up, we accumulate bad habits that will eventually have a knock-on effect. Your body can also give you more subtle messages about overdoing things, the best type of foods to eat and drinking enough water. All it takes is being in tune with your body.

FOR FURTHER REFLECTION

Psalm 32:8

DAY 108

Confide in God

One of the many names given to Christ is Wonderful Counsellor. We can take all our deepest problems to him knowing that he is non-partial, non-judgmental and offers complete confidentiality.

With God you don't have to explain yourself or your circumstances or your issues. He gets it. Don't bother trying to put on some kind of performance – just be real. He knows everything there is to know about you. He keeps the utmost confidentiality and you can be free to talk to him about absolutely anything. So open up and confide in him!

Isaiah 9:6
Matthew 6:6

Surprise Yourself

*'Count your blessings, name them one by one . . .
and it will surprise you what the Lord has done.' This
hymn, written by Johnson Oatman, speaks to each of
us of the importance of recognising God's goodness.*

We tend to count our miseries rather than our blessings. It's as if we default to focusing on the negative. Break out of this tendency by going against the flow. Recall the things that happened to you today. Think through how events actually worked in your favour – and be prepared for the surprises.

FOR FURTHER REFLECTION

Jeremiah 17:17

DAY 110

Don't Burn Out!

It's not work that wears us out, but worry, anxiety, fear and sadness. To God all your concerns are his concerns.

Emotional stress, trauma and anxiety are all negative feelings that sap the energy out of us. They drain and rob us of vital nutrients. Counteract this and save your energy by offloading to God. There's nothing so trivial that he won't pay attention to it. God just doesn't want us to become so overwhelmed that we lose sight of his unfailing power and strength.

FOR FURTHER REFLECTION

1 Peter 5:7

Meditate

Meditation enables us to calm down. Focus on this simple passage of scripture: 'Be still and know that I am God', and watch your body fall into relaxation.

Permission is given to us to be still. Find that quiet spot and just allow the demands of your day to be put on hold. God wants us to enter into his rest and think of him. Think of his goodness and power. Let your mind be free to explore the nature of God and see where it takes you. You can guarantee that every time you do this, you'll be on a completely different journey as you meditate on him.

FOR FURTHER REFLECTION

Psalm 46:10
Psalm 104:34

Claim the Promises

There are over three thousand promises in the Bible for help in time of need. Discover those hidden treasures – you're bound to find something that will comfort you in your present difficulties.

There's a biblical promise for every situation we find ourselves in. God's promises are sometimes conditional, based on our obedience toward him. Others are there for us simply to claim – such as: 'Call to me, and I will answer you, and show you great and mighty things' (Jeremiah 33:3). The only thing required of us here is simply to call to him. God doesn't ask too much of us, but the returns and rewards are unlimited. Not only that, but God always keeps his promises! You've got nothing to lose.

FOR FURTHER REFLECTION

2 Peter 1:4
Joshua 21:45

Take Time Out

*Today, make time to relax. Don't rush from one
task to another. Reflect on the goodness of God and
say a simple prayer of thanksgiving.*

You are spending energy on things you don't need to. You think some things are important when they're not. You have worries about things he's already taken care of. Let God's presence be your shelter and refuge – the place where you recover and feel safe and secure. Rest there and let him replenish you.

FOR FURTHER REFLECTION

Mark 6:31

Rejoice

*The psalmist declares: 'This is the day
that the Lord has made; we will rejoice and
be glad in it.'*

Today is a new day. There are new possibilities, hopes and blessings to be found. There are also people in your life and those you may never see again who will be impacted by you in some way. Today can be the day you sow seeds of promises and instil happiness in someone's life. It may also be a day when you learn something new about yourself. There are so many opportunities today. So make it count!

FOR FURTHER REFLECTION

Psalm 118:24

Be Optimistic

For every disappointment in our lives,
there are more than a hundred blessings.
Put your life into perspective!

If someone tells you to walk into a house and try to find imperfections – chipped paint, shoddy workmanship, worn-out furniture – what will your mind do when you walk in? Focus on the flaws. But if you've been told to find what's beautiful and delightful to you, your eyes will be drawn to those things instead. The same thing happens in our lives every day. Be someone who sees good things in the present and bright possibilities for change in the future. God puts them all around you.

FOR FURTHER REFLECTION

Psalm 107:38
Psalm 146:5–6

Remember the Sabbath

The Sabbath is God's gift to us. It's our opportunity to rest; to stop our regular work and become in tune with our creator.

God gave us a gift of time – one day in seven God tells us to stop from our work and labours and enjoy a time of rest. If God, who created us, saw that this was important for our lives, then that's something to take notice of. Many spend hundreds of pounds on consultants to diagnose their malady and all they are told is to take a day off and rest. God gives us that advice for free!

FOR FURTHER REFLECTION

Genesis 2:1–3
Exodus 20:8–11

Offload

Whatever challenge you're facing today, remember that nothing is too hard for God. Talk to him about it. Tell him what you are worried about, then leave it with him and watch what happens.

God knows the issues you're facing and he says to you: 'I have grace for all that you are encountering and far more than you will ever experience.' God accepts you exactly as you are. He wants to position you for healing and growth, and he's promised that if you cast all your cares upon him he will sustain you.

FOR FURTHER REFLECTION

Jeremiah 33:3
Psalm 55:22

Don't Despair

*We all feel lonely and vulnerable at times,
but remember God says: 'I will never leave you
nor forsake you.'*

Whether you get lonely living by yourself, or even in a crowd, there's something about isolation that messes with our perspective. Questions feel heavier and fear grips more tightly. The devil wants us to get isolated so that we forget all about God. But when we bring other people in we see things differently – our issues are not nearly as dark and hopeless as we had thought. Ask God to work through your relationships, to guide you with truth and wisdom and to strengthen you with his presence.

FOR FURTHER REFLECTION

Psalm 46:1
Hebrews 13:5

Set Yourself Free

*Forgive yourself! Yes, you made mistakes
and wrong decisions, and may even have rebelled.
But don't hold this against yourself perpetually.
Forgive and set yourself free from the bondage
of past guilt.*

It seems as though the hardest person to forgive is ourselves. We tend to be harder on ourselves than on those who have offended us. Deep-seated issues where you may have let someone down or failed to help when needed rub at the core of consciousness. Rather than allowing these past mistakes to rule your present life, you have to let them go and embrace the forgiveness that God has already given you. Don't be tied to your past failures. Do yourself a favour, forgive yourself and be rid of any guilt and shame.

FOR FURTHER REFLECTION

Psalm 51

Seek God First

*The main purpose of life is not just to be happy
or satisfied, but to know God for ourselves.
If we seek to do this, we will be happy and satisfied.*

The whole purpose of life is to know God and to follow his teachings. When we do this we have a blueprint for what happiness is really all about. God understands this world better than you do and is more powerful than anything in it. He knows how you can live fully and freely and he's endlessly generous in enabling you to do that. The next time you're anxious, stay close to his heart and let him reach every part of your life. Keep saying: 'I believe you can help me in this moment.' As you look out to the days ahead of you, tell him: 'I want to live in the joy and happiness you made me for.'

FOR FURTHER REFLECTION

Matthew 6:33

DAY 121

Trust in God's Direction

Let go of the past with its mistakes and mishaps.
Your future lies ahead with untapped new
opportunities. Move forward in the full assurance
God will make a new path for you!

It's so easy to dwell on past mistakes. Regrets can plague our minds: we say to ourselves: 'If only I had done it a different way', or 'I wish I had never responded in the way that I did.' We all have regrets but we can't let them perpetually rule our lives. You have to let the hurt of past mistakes go, forgive yourself for what you did and embrace the new path God wants you to take. He says, 'Let me show you how to be well. You need care! I will help you and I know the right path to take – follow me.' God is your nurturing caregiver and wise guide – ask him to provide the nourishment and help you need today.

FOR FURTHER REFLECTION

Philippians 3:12–13

De-stress

When stress threatens your concentration,
picture yourself in a relaxing environment.
Take a deep breath, inhale thoughts of peace and
calm, then exhale all your anxieties and tensions.
Do this now for a few minutes.

You have to take control of your negative feelings and emotions in the present situation. If not, you can become overwhelmed with the build-up of pressure and tension that constantly knock on the door of your heart. Take stock of how you're feeling. Be in tune with your mood and emotions, then respond accordingly. Taking deep breaths help clear the mind by getting added oxygen into the brain cells. Then breathe out the very thought that's troubling you. Whatever practical steps you find helpful to regain control of your composure – do them. Then de-stress and get on top of your situation.

FOR FURTHER REFLECTION

Mark 6:31

Don't Give Up

*If Christ can calm the turbulent sea, then he is
more than able to say to your storm: 'Peace, be still!'*

On average thunderstorms or heavy rain last for an average of thirty minutes. Within an hour you can see a complete contrast. After a storm, blue skies become a welcome sight and before long the thunderstorm is soon forgotten. No storm lasts for ever – it will come to an end. The same is true of the storms of life. We all go through them and for some, the dark clouds and rain seem to last for ever. We are not promised that life will be blue skies and sunshine all the time, but we can learn to adopt a positive outlook in the midst of our storms. Keep looking for the ray of light at the end of the tunnel. If God brought you to it, he will bring you through it.

FOR FURTHER REFLECTION

Mark 4:39
Psalm 107:29

Start with Prayer

Begin the day with prayer. Make that your first duty.
Your mind will be refreshed and ready to face
life's demands.

Beginning the day with prayer is like checking in with God before you meet with anyone else. You don't know what your day will bring or what potential mishaps may lie ahead. Check in with God first to ensure he's got you protected throughout the day – this is not something to take for granted. Put God first and he will take care of all of your other priorities within the day. Then go through your day with the full assurance God is with you and has got you covered!

FOR FURTHER REFLECTION

Psalm 55:17

Take a Second Look

Try looking at your surroundings through the eyes of a child. Children will notice the most amazing sights, full of colour and imagination, that you've been passing by all this time.

Children see things we don't. If you have ever been for a walk with children, have you noticed how they point out things that you were oblivious of? As you walk along the street, they see the tabby cat asleep by the tree, the colourful butterfly circling in the sky, the falling sycamore leaves spinning like helicopters to the ground. Yet we walk right past these little object lessons of life. It's noticing these little things that makes our journey meaningful and draws our attention to God's marvellous creation. So be more observant next time and see what new things you can notice.

FOR FURTHER REFLECTION

Matthew 18:3

DAY 126

Reflect on Your Day

At the end of your day, take time to reflect on what you appreciated the most. Then take time to give thanks to God.

We experience a lot of things throughout the day – little moments that bring a smile to our faces, or something someone said that made us think. Little things that make a strong, positive impact when they occur can easily be forgotten by the end of the day. However, taking time to reflect on your day and bring to memory these moments of influence allows you to solidify them in your mind. It also enables you to have a more meaningful conversation with God about what you appreciated through your day. This simple act allows you to be mindful of what people say or do, enabling you to be more appreciative.

FOR FURTHER REFLECTION

Deuteronomy 28:6

Look Heavenward

Christ came to live with us in lowly surroundings, so that one day we can live with him in heavenly surroundings.

We will never really know here on earth what heaven is like. Our greatest thoughts or imagination are just too clouded with imperfection. Whatever you think heaven is like, it is a billion to the power of a billion much better – and that is still an understatement. Right now we can only imagine how majestic and beautiful heaven really is. The good news is that one day we will know. Christ has made it all possible by leaving that perfect place to come to this imperfect place, yet lived a perfect life so we who are imperfect will one day also live in perfection. Now that's something to look forward to!

FOR FURTHER REFLECTION

Luke 2:12–16

Don't Put Yourself Down

Never say: 'I'm not good enough.'
If that's the case, then you're God's first mistake,
and God doesn't make mistakes.

Negative talk goes a long way and can settle deep in our subconscious. We are already bombarded with a lot of negative talk from other people each day, so why make it worse by putting yourself down? Don't say belittling things to yourself and never say you are not good enough. There may be things that you may not be skilled at or trained to do, but these are expected in life. You are good at something and that's all that matters. If you're still on a path to discovering what you are good at, just think of the things that you naturally enjoy doing and come easily to you and focus on them.

FOR FURTHER REFLECTION

Zechariah 2:8

Open up to Joy

Joy comes from within and radiates out.
Think of things that you are grateful for and then see
how joy radiates from within you like a beacon.

The feeling of joy comes from you. It's what flows out from you based on how you perceive any given situation. God wants you to have the most joy you can possibly have and ultimately the source of joy comes from abiding in the Father's love and having a closeness with him. Joy doesn't come from a pain-free existence, or from having what the world values – it comes from the joyful one himself. Every time you choose the way of life, the way God calls good and right and beautiful, you take another step towards that big joy. So keep coming to him with an open heart full of faith, and let his joy be in you.

FOR FURTHER REFLECTION

Psalm 23:5

DAY 130

Create Special Moments

*The most memorable days may not necessarily
be those where something spectacular happens,
but those that bring simple pleasures, like relaxing
by a crackling fireside and watching the flames
dancing to and fro.*

Special moments don't have to be involve great financial expense. We don't have to do the extraordinary or spectacular. The greatest and most treasured memories can be achieved through simple things. It's about being mindful of what you're enjoying in the present. Notice the things you do within your day that bring you relaxation or a sense of calm. It may simply be relaxing in your favourite chair as you knit, read or meditate. Whatever it is, be mindful of how it makes you feel. A potential special moment can easily be taken for granted or passed by, simply because you haven't identified it as a special moment.

FOR FURTHER REFLECTION

Psalm 96:11–12

Hope in God

*Many people die with no hope. But worse still
are those living with no hope. Put your hope in God,
who promises something better one day soon.*

We don't have to amplify the negative and downplay the positive. We can choose hope instead of pessimism. We can notice and soak in God's goodness and let his love and words of promise fill our hearts. We can respond to him by saying: 'My hope is in you all day long.' If things are looking dark and dismal for you right now, be assured God is preparing amazing things. So let this anticipation spark hope and joy within you.

FOR FURTHER REFLECTION

Romans 15:13
Psalm 25:5

Become Childlike

The sound of children playing and laughing often brings a welcome smile. It reminds us how jubilant they can be in simple things. We still have a lot to learn from children about how we approach life.

Watch how children laugh. It doesn't take much to start them giggling and enjoying playful moments. Do you know how Jesus treated children? They felt pulled like a magnet to him and he couldn't have been happier about it. Can you imagine how much love, comfort and peace they must have felt in his presence? You are God's child and he wants you to enjoy him. So do that – run to your heavenly Father, talk to him, and when the occasion arrives, laugh out loud.

FOR FURTHER REFLECTION

Matthew 19:14

Take Ten Seconds of Time

*Today you have 86,400 seconds of time,
and it takes less than 10 seconds to make
a difference in someone else's life!*

How will you spend your day today? You may have work to do, a job to go to or assignments to complete, but we all have the same amount of time in a day. Yet it's the smallest things we can do that will make a huge difference to others: a simple smile, a warm hello, holding the door for someone, going out of your way to help a co-worker. Check in with your neighbour and see if there's anything you can do for them. Send an encouraging note, listen intently to someone, be the reason people feel cared for and supported. Let the love of God flow through you to someone – it takes less than 10 seconds.

FOR FURTHER REFLECTION

Lamentations 3:22–23

Appreciate God's Goodness

Every day you are at the centre of God's thoughts.
He says: 'For I know the thoughts that I think towards
you . . . thoughts of peace and not of evil, to give
you a future and a hope.'

Nothing and no one can change the character of our open and infinite God. He has no skewed motives, no corrupt desires, no darkness at all. He is perfect, pure and lovely. If you have any challenges in your life, he will find a way to use them to carry out his purposes and to shape you in beauty and bring blessings. It takes time and you won't be able to understand it along the way, but God will accomplish his 'good and acceptable and perfect will'. Don't let anything – not the pain or questions or difficulties of this life – convince you otherwise.

FOR FURTHER REFLECTION

Jeremiah 29:11
Romans 12:2
Psalm 100

Remember You're Special

The whole mission of Christ is to 'seek and save' you.
Christ left all the glories and splendour of heaven just
to find and rescue you. It's because he does not
want to lose you.

God wants us to know that his promises have the ultimate staying power. When the one he loves turns away from him, God pursues that person no matter what they have done! Deep intimacy, tender affection, undying commitment, never-ending forgiveness – God's heart for you is unfailing always and for ever. So please believe with all your heart that in God's eyes, you are a person he so highly values that nothing will prevent him from loving you.

FOR FURTHER REFLECTION

Luke 19:10

Let Jesus In

*When Jesus comes into your life, he brings with
him his calming influence. What a bonus!*

Maybe you feel like you're running out of steam to tackle the
next thing. Maybe you're concerned something bad is coming
around the corner. Maybe you're hung up on your weaknesses
and afraid of making mistakes. Whether you're weary, worried or
burdened with cares, you need to come to God and receive his
abundant, unconditional love. When you're worn out, his power is
incomparable and miraculous. So let Jesus into your heart today
and allow him to be the director of your life.

FOR FURTHER REFLECTION

Matthew 11:28
Psalm 29:11

Bridge the Gap

Is there someone you need to be reconciled with?
Think about what steps you can take today to
bring restoration.

Jesus desires for us to be united. He prayed that: 'they may be made perfect in one, and that the world may know that you have sent me, and have loved them as you have loved me' (John 17:23). How tragic it would be if we let petty issues and frustrations keep us from the amazing destiny God has for us! Remember, it's God who enables you to live and breathe and get through your day, so we all depend on him for survival. Don't let separation between you and someone else hinder either of you from living a free and joyful life. So make that first move – you have nothing to lose but everything to gain!

FOR FURTHER REFLECTION

Matthew 5:24

Let the Shepherd Lead

Psalm 23 is a calming passage of scripture:
'He makes me to lie down in green pastures; he leads
me beside the still waters, he restores my soul.'

If there's one passage of scripture that epitomises what calm is all about, it's Psalm 23. The imagery of the words used leads you to a vision of peace: 'green pastures', 'still waters', 'restores my soul'. God is a caregiver; the best one you'll ever have. He's a shepherd who watches over all his sheep – even though they are sometimes stubborn, senseless or distracted. He patiently stays with them, guiding them away from dangers into nourishing spaces. He leads them to life-giving water and gives them new strength. It only makes sense that if Jesus is our shepherd and we are the often senseless, stubborn sheep, that we let the Good Shepherd lead us into green pastures and allow him to nourish and sustain us as we go through life.

FOR FURTHER REFLECTION

Psalm 23

Replace Fear with Joy

The proclamation of Christ's birth to the shepherds by the angel was in the words: 'Do not be afraid, for behold, I bring you good tidings of great joy' (Luke 2:9). These words still ring true today for you in your life!

When God proclaims the truth with a blessing, be assured that the promise remains for ever. When God blesses, there's nothing that can be done to reverse it. So get ready and start claiming all the precious promises in the Bible. They are all still applicable today. Sharing good news with others is an exciting task, and it's a joy to see the other person's expression of happiness and surprise! Now imagine the same angel declaring the same message to you that he gave to the shepherds in Bethlehem: 'Do not fear – I've good news for you that will bring great joy. The saviour that was born in Bethlehem as a baby is the same saviour who wants to rescue you from sin and all its effects!'

FOR FURTHER REFLECTION

Luke 2:18

Tame Your Tongue

*The tongue is a powerful weapon that can
permanently hurt or destroy someone. We need
to control the words that come out of our mouths
and ensure we use our tongues to encourage,
uplift and spread positivity.*

Guard your tongue, because it's the one organ of the body that can emit words that can either destroy or build up. There used to be a song sung at school: 'Sticks and stones will break my bones, but words will never hurt me.' How wrong that is – words can indeed hurt us and perhaps have a more lasting effect than sticks and stones. On a more positive note, we have many opportunities to use our words to inspire, encourage and instil hope in people's lives. If our hearts are right, what we say will be right. So let the change begin in our hearts.

FOR FURTHER REFLECTION

James 1:19–26; 3:1–12
1 Peter 3:10
Colossians 4:6

Go Forward in Confidence

*Be assured that angels are on a mission
to watch over you today!*

God's not standing opposite you. He's standing by your side. He is not against you. He is for you. You are his precious creation and he calls you wonderful and lovely. He's given you his Spirit of power to live in you, to guide you to help you in every way. So you can trust him. Align yourself with him every day and let his Spirit reign in you so you can move forward with the greatest confidence.

FOR FURTHER REFLECTION

Psalm 34:7

Avoid Negativity

Don't focus on the one negative comment or wrong thing that happens today, compared to all the positive things that happen.

It's a common tendency. A hundred positive things could happen in your day and then one negative incident takes place. Then the ninety-nine good things that occurred are swept to the side as we sink into despondency over that one thing. We need to turn the tables. Don't let the one negative incident mar the beauty of your day. We have to look above negativities and remove their stubborn tendencies to dominate our thinking. We can only dwell on one thing at a time, so edge out anything that's not wholesome, uplifting or positive and leave no space for anything that doesn't serve a positive purpose.

FOR FURTHER REFLECTION

Ephesians 5:20

Be Courageous

The word 'courage' comes from the French word coeur, meaning 'heart'. If God promised it, believe it and move forward despite the obstacles, and don't lose heart.

When God says: 'Be strong and courageous', he has something important for you to do and he wants you to join him. There will be challenges before you and obstacles you will have to face. There will be hard things for you to do. So be brave. Be who he made you to be. Go forward in faith! Do what he made you to do. God gives you a spirit of power, not fear. He has equipped you, positioned you and called you and now he says, 'Go'. Go with great faith, thinking of his power – be brave and move forward!

FOR FURTHER REFLECTION

2 Chronicles 15:7
Isaiah 35:3–4
Deuteronomy 31:6

Inspire Others

Use what you have to inspire and enrich the lives of others. Your life stories and experiences are invaluable treasures that can be used to bless and encourage.

Everything you go through serves two main purposes. The first is to teach you life lessons that will guide you, and the second is to share those lessons with others. Even the smallest things we experience can make a huge difference to others. There are certain negative experiences you should avoid going through, having heard from others how they suffered through them. Learn from the life stories of those who come into contact with you. Their hard and challenging experiences should be a warning to avoid going down a similar path. Similarly, another person's triumph and perseverance in achieving their aims can inspire you to make the same efforts to help reach your goals and desires.

FOR FURTHER REFLECTION

1 Timothy 5:1–2

Give Your Worries to God

Worry is not productive. It won't pay bills or solve problems. You don't add one day to your life by worrying, but you may age prematurely. So do yourself a favour – trust God with the situation and leave the outcome to him.

What are you worried about? What's causing you to feel distressed right now? As you think through those issues, ask yourself: 'What can I do about them?' You will find that there's very little you can actually do. What worry actually says to God is: 'Lord, you're not big enough to deal with this situation, so I'm going to deal with it myself.' Therein lies the struggle worry brings to each of us, because often the things that plague our minds are issues we can do nothing about. So do the best thing – relieve yourself of unnecessary tension and transfer all your cares and worries to God. You know he can deal with them, so just let him be God!

FOR FURTHER REFLECTION

Matthew 6:27
Isaiah 26:3

Channel Your Mind

*Instead of trying to get rid of negative
thoughts which only keep you focused on them,
fill your mind with positive scriptural thoughts such as:
'No weapon formed against me shall prosper!'*

Find an encouraging scripture in the Bible – one that brings you great comfort and assurance. Now commit that scripture to memory. Whenever a nagging thought enters your mind, counteract it by verbally quoting that scripture. Soon an association will develop between the nagging thought and the scripture, and you'll find that the thought will dissipate and disappear. You can defeat any negative thought with the Word of God. Give it a try and see what happens!

FOR FURTHER REFLECTION

Matthew 4:1–11
Isaiah 54:17

Focus on What's Good

When things are not going well in your life,
you can choose to focus on fear or faith, problems
or solutions, despair or hope.

Your thoughts are completely under your control. What you decide to dwell on is up to you. Yes, negative and debilitating thoughts may arise, but you don't have to allow them to dominate your thinking. You are what you think, so for every fearful thought, think of a way out through faith. For every problem that seems insurmountable, there's always a solution to counteract it. For every despairing moment, there's always a hopeful outcome to embrace. You never need feel defeated!

FOR FURTHER REFLECTION

Philippians 4:8

Rise Above Temporary Setbacks

*We don't have to look very far to find things
to complain about, but when you focus on God,
he lifts you above your circumstances and gives
you an aerial view of the bigger picture of
what's happening in your life.*

Your perception always changes when you view things from a different angle. Sometimes we bury our heads in the sand, not wanting to face reality. We feel cornered and can only see approaching turmoil. We feel trapped in darkness with no discernment of any light of day. That's because we're only focusing on the problem. You need to look beyond the issue at hand and look upwards. Remember God is there for you and let him elevate you above the present situation. You will then begin to see the sunshine above the clouds.

FOR FURTHER REFLECTION

Psalm 56:3–4

The Joy of Heaven

Tears may flow from your hardships and griefs in life, but there will be a time when God 'will wipe away every tear from our eyes' (Revelation 7:17). There will be no more grief and sadness, and our only tears will be tears of joy.

Today we see the effects of living in a sinful world all around us: death, suffering, pain, hardship and sadness, to name just a few. However, a better tomorrow is promised to each of us. It's a hope that can lift us above our temporary setbacks to look forward to something better. The day will come when sin and its effects will finally be destroyed. Jesus said: 'Behold I make all things new.' A better day is coming!

FOR FURTHER REFLECTION

Revelation 21:5

Admit Your Faults

*Confession really is good for the soul. It purges
us from the burden of guilt and shame. The good news
is that we can confess directly to our heavenly Father,
who hears and understands all things.*

It's hard to admit to ourselves when we are wrong. It can be harder still to confess to others that we were at fault. It takes an authentic person to recognise that their action or behaviour was unacceptable and admit that to the offended. However, it's the kind of attitude that helps us grow. It certainly clears our minds and purifies our souls. So don't act as if you're infallible. When you're wrong, admit it, apologise and learn from your mistakes.

FOR FURTHER REFLECTION

1 John 1:9

Stick with God's Plan

God is 'the Alpha and the Omega, the beginning and the end'. It is because he knows the outcome of our trials that he says: 'Trust me.' It's because he's already seen the victorious outcome that he says: 'Don't give up!'

It's because we can't see the outcome that fear can take hold of us. Our minds can have a field day conjuring up different, usually negative, scenarios of how things might play out. 'What will happen if . . . ?', 'Who will take care of me when . . . ?', 'How will I get through this?' These thoughts have no real answer, so the mind tries to fill the gaps. However, God loves to fill those gaps – he's already seen the outcome. He knows the better person you will become when you get through it. He just wants you to trust him through the process and with the outcome.

FOR FURTHER REFLECTION

Ephesians 1:11
Revelation 22:13

Hold On

It's during the testing times that you will discover that God is good and faithful. He may stretch you, but never beyond your breaking point. His plan is for you to come out of this experience stronger for what's next on his agenda.

Every experience you go through sets you up for the next encounter. At the time you can't see that. You think about how you're going to get through this present situation. But in life nothing really happens for no reason. There's always something you can learn from what you're presently experiencing, no matter how tough it is. As hard as it may be, God is with you every step of the way and sometimes he carries you through your difficult time. When it's all over, you will wonder how you got through it.

FOR FURTHER REFLECTION

Deuteronomy 7:9

Hang on in There

Regardless of how badly you have failed or how often you have failed, God won't give up on you. So don't give up on yourself!

It takes courage to get back up again having failed, and even more courage when we've failed at the same thing again. There are some things you may have to admit are not for you to pursue, but there is no limit to the number of times you need get back up and keep going. God, who knows about you with all your darkest secrets and hidden skeletons, still loves and adores you. He will never change his mind about you and you can never be separated from him. So know this – God's not going anywhere. Just hang on in there and accept it!

FOR FURTHER REFLECTION

Psalm 3:2–6

Bask in God's Love

Human love is often flawed. It keeps a record of our mistakes and shortcomings, but God has no such list! His love cannot be measured.

Human love often falls short. God's love, however, is perfect. When someone in your life whom you thought loved you turns away from you, it's a hard thing to deal with. But that's where we see the limitations of human love. The only person who can truly love us the way we need to be loved is Jesus. His love fills that void which no one else can fill.

FOR FURTHER REFLECTION

1 John 4:8
Song of Solomon 8:7

Claim What's Lost

Whatever life has taken from you, God can restore.
He may not give you exactly what you want,
but he'll give you what's best.

God knows what's best for us. What we want and think we need may not marry up with what God thinks is best for us. However, what God provides far outweighs what we thought we wanted. Sometimes when it seems as if our prayers are not answered, it's because God is actually working on an upgrade to what we ask. So if your health is impaired, your finances are dwindling or something precious has been lost, God has already taken this into consideration and has a got a plan to sustain you, leading to an even closer walk with him.

FOR FURTHER REFLECTION

Joel 2:25

Belly Laugh

The best type of laughing occurs when it comes deep down from the belly. Find something to laugh about today and really let go!

There's laughing and there's real laughing! Have you ever experienced that deep belly laugh where it seems all inhibitions are set aside? You laugh as if you just don't care. Then when you've finished, don't you just feel good inside? There are many health benefits from doing that, but laughing out loud is remedial in many other ways. It may be that you're not the type of person to laugh this way, especially in public, but there's nothing stopping you from doing so in the privacy of your own home. You go through so much, so find something that you know will make you laugh and let go!

FOR FURTHER REFLECTION

Philippians 4:4

Treasure Simple Moments

*Little things, like listening to the rain outside
while watching the drops roll down the window,
can often bring on a calming experience.*

It's the simple things that carry great weight. Never under-estimate the seemingly mundane or insignificant occurrences of everyday life. They are there all the time, waiting for you to be mindful of them. They wait for you to pay attention so they can dazzle you with their enchantment. They want to be noticed so they can wield a calming influence in your life. Look around where you are right now, or look outside the window – what can you see that gives you a sense of peace and calm? Focus on it.

FOR FURTHER REFLECTION

1 Thessalonians 5:8
Matthew 6:21

Act Conscientiously

*A calming influence comes when you know you've
done the right thing, no matter what people think.*

You can't please people all the time. When you seek to please others you will undoubtedly compromise what you believe to be true. There are times when, for the sake of what's right, you will have to act in accordance with your conscience. Ask yourself: 'What is the appropriate way to proceed in this matter?' It may be that not everyone will be happy with your decision, but the main thing will be that you have a clear mind, knowing that you did what was right.

FOR FURTHER REFLECTION

2 Kings 22:2

DAY 159

Seek Godly Counsel

Whenever you go through a challenging time, always ask: 'Lord, what do you want me to learn from this experience?'

There are always lessons to be learned from the experiences we go through. In the midst of a trial, however, that may not be the first thought in our minds. We simply want to get through to the other side. When we pause however and ask: 'Lord, what do you want me to learn from this?', we begin to ask questions that will put a different perspective on what we're encountering. This enables us to recognise that although things may be difficult right now, they will serve a higher purpose.

FOR FURTHER REFLECTION

James 1:5
Romans 8:28

Soak It Away

*Whenever you're feeling low, run a hot bath,
add some relaxing salts and your favourite bubble
bath and soak away your worries.*

The thought of a nice hot, relaxing bath gives a welcoming picture of relaxation and calm. For some, however, having a bath may seem like a luxury. Most houses have just showers or a small tub. The idea is doing something that takes your thoughts and mind away from the hustle and bustle of the day and allows you to let off steam. Relaxation is vital to the soul to experience calm. So, whatever your situation, find something relaxing to do and give yourself some 'me time'.

FOR FURTHER REFLECTION

Matthew 11:28–29

DAY 161

Be Comforted

The Greek word for 'comforter' is parakletos,
meaning 'the one who comes alongside to help you'.
There will never be a day when you won't need
God to be by your side.

'You'll never walk alone' is a song associated with a popular football team. The words, however, really have their truest meaning in relation to God's promise of his Comforter. Jesus declared: 'And I will pray the Father, and he shall give you another Comforter, that he may abide with you for ever.' The Holy Spirit is that comforter, and one of his roles is to be alongside us in our everyday life. That's why the scriptures declare: 'I will never leave you nor forsake you.'

FOR FURTHER REFLECTION

John 14:16
2 Corinthians 1:4
Isaiah 66:13

Share Your Testimony

*Don't downplay the importance of your faith.
When it naturally fits a conversation, talk about the
good things God has done for you. Let others see
the joy and purpose in your life.*

Too often we shy away from telling others about the hope that we have within us. We can even sit and listen to others' views and opinions about different things in life and yet we stay silent. If something means so much to you and is the source of your joy and peace, can you really keep that to yourself? You never know – someone you meet may be struggling with a problem, and what they really need to hear is something that can reassure them. That's where you come in. Don't feel your faith is too personal and should only be kept for yourself – let someone else into your secret and share the hope!

FOR FURTHER REFLECTION

1 Corinthians 9:22

Pray Every Day

God wants you to talk to him every day. Tell him about everything you're going through – he wants to be your faithful companion for always!

Prayer is simply talking to God as a friend. There are no real rules about how you pray. Get a picture of God in your mind – something that you remember him doing in the Bible, like Jesus sitting with the children, healing the blind man, or whatever you can come up with. Then use that picture as the basis of who you talk to when you pray. That way your prayers become a lot more personal.

FOR FURTHER REFLECTION

Proverbs 3:6
Proverbs 16:3

Keep a Clear Mind

*The moment you begin to feel anxious about
something, take the problem straight to God in prayer.
By releasing the weight of it you can have a clear
mind to hear God's answer to the problem.*

Don't allow your mind to ruminate over a problem. The more
you dwell on it, the larger it gets. The idea is to offload it immediately by sharing it with God. When it festers and develops,
you become overwhelmed and it becomes a much bigger task to
handle. It is said that a problem shared is a problem halved, so by
sharing it with God, you're cutting up the problem into bite-sized
pieces. The goal is to not allow the problem to become so big that
it clouds your mind and you can't think straight.

FOR FURTHER REFLECTION

Philippians 4:6–7

When God Calls, Move!

*When you feel prompted to offer words of comfort
to someone, don't hesitate. You've been moved to
do so to meet God's timing not yours.*

'A word fitly spoken is like apples of gold in settings of silver' (Proverbs 25:11). This scripture reminds us how saying something at the right time to bring encouragement and hope to someone is of great value. It doesn't have to be a sermon – just one or two words that hold weight can make a significant difference. Bear in mind also that when God puts you into a situation to encourage someone, he will provide the thoughts and words for you to speak.

FOR FURTHER REFLECTION

Proverbs 25:11
Proverbs 11:30

Trust Blindly

Some things in life you will never know the answer to, or the reason why they happened. That's when you need to implicitly trust that God knows best.

Answers to our questions about certain occurrences in life are not always guaranteed. If anything negative happens to us, our default response is wanting to know why. We want closure and clarity. When answers can't be found, know that God is still in control. He sees everything and understands the anguish of your heart, so allow him to take you through unexplained circumstances where the only thing you can do is trust all things will work together for good.

FOR FURTHER REFLECTION

Romans 8:28
Deuteronomy 29:29

Stay Blessed

*It wasn't luck that gave you what you got,
it's because you're blessed! Take a moment to
give God the credit.*

Today the phrase 'I'm blessed' is becoming more common in everyday language. The word, however, has deep spiritual roots. It means a favour or gift bestowed by God, or the involvement of God's providence in an unexpected way. The real key to its meaning is the recipient's recognition that everything they have comes from God. Therefore for a believer in God to say 'I'm blessed' highlights the one who gives the blessings. By virtue of being a child of God, every day and every moment of the day you are blessed!

FOR FURTHER REFLECTION

Deuteronomy 28

Consider Yourself Successful

God will never see you as a failure.
You're always cherished, valued and highly favoured.

In God's eyes there are no losers, in heaven's eyes no hopeless cause. When God created you, you were deemed 'fearfully and wonderfully made'. Because God never makes any mistakes you can account yourself accepted and valued. While as humans we judge each other based on how we look, talk, walk and numerous other factors, God sees you simply as his child. When God aligns himself with you, you can't lose!

FOR FURTHER REFLECTION

Psalm 139:14–15

Get Re-directed

God can turn your rejection to re-direction.
When one door closes, he will always open another one.
Watch out for it!

Life has its unexpected turns. One moment you can be in a stable job earning a decent income, the next moment you're made redundant at work and facing a financial crisis. Things change without much notice and that's the reality of life – it comes with unexpected twists and turns. However, if you commit your life and future to God's hands, when it seems like there's no way forward he will always provide a new way for you. Don't let the despair of a closed door impair your vision of the new door that's about to open!

FOR FURTHER REFLECTION

Revelation 3:8

Pray First

*There's nothing better than to begin your day
with prayer. When you make Christ your first priority,
he will take care of all your other priorities.*

Mounting tasks and assignments for the day can often over-whelm us. There may also be pressing issues that need to be dealt with. The best way to counteract this is to put your day before God before you do anything else. Tell him about all the things you have to face and how you feel about them. Ask God for guidance and direction. Even if you have nothing planned for the day, simply asking for protection is the least that you can pray for.

FOR FURTHER REFLECTION

Matthew 6:33

Draw Closer to God

*God never changes. His love for you will always
be the same regardless of how far you have strayed.
Let his love draw you closer to him.*

When we feel distant from God, it's not him who has moved away, but us. God never turns away. It's us who drift away and before we know it, the current of life's pressures has taken us further away than we realised. God wants us to turn to him – that's all we can do. We will naturally draw close to God by simply refusing to turn away from him.

FOR FURTHER REFLECTION

James 4:8

DAY 172

Be Patient

Waiting time is not wasted time. God is working on both ends of the line: he's getting you ready for 'it' and 'it' ready for you.

Waiting time is preparation time. To every prayer the answer from God could be 'yes', 'no' or 'wait'. The waiting process to your prayers may be longer than you expect – that's the hardest part. You have to trust God with the process. Remember that God's timing is perfect and he will give you what he knows will benefit you at the right time and place.

FOR FURTHER REFLECTION

Psalm 27:14

DAY 173

Endure

*Challenging times will always come, but don't despair:
the greater the conflict, the greater the conquest;
the harder the battle, the sweeter the victory.*

The greatest victories arrive after the hardest battles. It's when you feel you can't carry on any further or deal with the pressures placed on you that holding on and persevering through to the end yields the greatest rewards. The first reward is that you kept going and never gave up; the second reward is the greater strength of character you've developed as a result of it.

FOR FURTHER REFLECTION

1 Samuel 17:47
2 Chronicles 20:15

Be Brave

*Letting go of something you know is harmful to you
is the bravest step toward growth. You may yearn for it,
but stay strong: you will soon see the benefits.*

God gives you a spirit of power, not fear. Let that spirit of power drive your thoughts and actions. He will enable you to do hard and difficult things. So be brave. God made you to be an overcomer – don't feel defeated. You can let go of the things that you've been entangled with over the years. You don't have to feel helpless and resigned to a continual life of failure. Allow the power of God to equip and position you for success.

FOR FURTHER REFLECTION

Deuteronomy 31:6
Revelation 3:11
James 1:3

Don't Let Feelings Be the Boss

Your feelings can often change like the weather.
Avoid making permanent decisions based on
temporary feelings.

If your circumstances have you bouncing from confusion to anger to fear, remember that God is working in invisible ways. You can't see all the good he's doing, but you can trust he's doing it. So live by what you believe rather than by what you feel. Hold on to his promises and truth instead of the mood of the moment. Trust him to be your powerful, ever-present helper. Say in your prayers: 'Lord, I want what you say – not my feelings – to guide me.'

FOR FURTHER REFLECTION

Ephesians 4:26
2 Corinthians 5:7

Esteem One Another

Words of affirmation will always create an atmosphere of calm and tranquillity.

Criticism of one another often prevails within our human interaction. It can be done subtly by complaining, disrespecting, belittling or making fun of someone. What comes out of our mouth has the power for life or death. We speak and the words can never be returned. That's why it's so important to watch what you say. Find something positive to say about someone. Let them know how valued they are and ensure they leave your presence feeling better than when they arrived.

FOR FURTHER REFLECTION

1 Thessalonians 5:11

Stay on God's Side

If God is for you, who can be against you?
Go forth today with that assurance!

You have the greatest defender by your side. He is immutable, the undisputed champion of all time. He's never lost a battle, never failed in handling a dilemma, never been overwhelmed by any situation. Yes, that's the kind of defender you have on your side. No one can faze him, nothing can shock him and nobody can tire him. We have someone who is always with us, will never forsake us and will never leave us. That's the kind of God that you serve – never go through your day without him!

FOR FURTHER REFLECTION

Romans 8:31

DAY 178

Be Grateful

Appreciate the 'now' moments of your life.
A better tomorrow always starts with a grateful today.

Enjoying those special moments is the goal of life. You can achieve this by simply being more mindful of what you have around you. You have to be able to identify things that bring you happiness and contentment. Sometimes you may look back at a memory and recall how much fun that day was, but at the time you never saw it that way. So capture those moments and say: 'What I'm experiencing right now is a happy moment.'

FOR FURTHER REFLECTION

Psalm 118:24
Ephesians 5:16

Appreciate Your Differences

You are special because you're unique.
Instead of comparing yourself with others,
discover your God-given differences.

You're also special because God said so. He created you with a unique set of blueprints that are encoded in your DNA. There's only one person like you. Amazingly, there are things that only you can do effectively. You have particular abilities given to you by God to create your own space in the world and do something that will ultimately give glory to him.

FOR FURTHER REFLECTION

Isaiah 64:8
Jeremiah 1:4–5

Be Comforted

The act of comforting someone is reciprocal.
When you comfort someone, you yourself
become comforted.

It's easy when going though challenging times just to think about the suffering you are going through. Our minds are introspective. We focus on our own pain. But when we reach out of ourselves and put aside our own feelings to focus on others, something remarkable happens within us. We are reminded not only that someone else may be in a far worse position than we are, but that the mere act of reaching out to comfort brings healing to us too.

FOR FURTHER REFLECTION

Isaiah 40:1
1 Thessalonians 4:18

Replenish Yourself

*When was the last time you flew a kite,
strolled by a lake, relaxed on a park bench or
just enjoyed the singing of birds?*

There's only so much you can give when helping others before your own energy levels begin to falter. To be an effective support to others you have to look after yourself. Self-care is all about guarding yourself from external circumstances that can deplete you emotionally, physically and mentally. That's why recharging those energy levels are so important. Keep topping up your own well so you can provide a more effective service of watering the lives of others.

FOR FURTHER REFLECTION

Isaiah 40:31

Put God First

*Don't make God the last resort for help.
Make him your first 'go to' person and reduce
the time wasted in worry.*

For every minute of worry you go through, an immeasurable amount of vital resources is being depleted from your soul. Worry is like an aggressive thorn that tears away at the healthy plant, preventing it from growing and flourishing. The longer you hold on to it, the more destruction it will cause, preventing any blossoming in your life. Do yourself a favour – just like any thorn or weed you see emerging, nip it off straight away. Prune it out by taking it to the Master Creator of all life and letting him handle it. Then you will see the petals and flowers of your life emerging once again.

FOR FURTHER REFLECTION

**Philippians 4:6
Matthew 6:25–34**

Claim God's Promises

*We can never keep all our promises.
But God is 100 per cent faithful. Every one of
God's promises are 'yes' in Christ.*

Promises are there for you to claim in the Bible. There are thousands of them just waiting for you to discover. They are dotted throughout scripture and are freely available to everyone. Unlike humans, God always keeps his promises as long as they are in line with his will for you. Next time you see a biblical promise you want to claim, put your finger on the verse of scripture and pray over it. Declare to God that you want to claim this promise for the situation you are in. Pray in faith, believing that God will apply that promise to your life.

FOR FURTHER REFLECTION

2 Corinthians 1:20

Remain Confident

Whatever circumstances may arise, you can face them with peace and confidence knowing that God is with you.

Fear will say you're not good enough. But you have to say no to fear with confidence – refuse to let it diminish your view of who you are and who you can become. God made you so you could pursue the works he called you to do. Some failure along the way isn't going to change that. God is able to empower you to grow and be resilient. Don't underestimate him! So push fear out of the way and be confident.

FOR FURTHER REFLECTION

Hebrews 10:35–36

Accept God's Love

There is nothing you can do to make God love you more. There is nothing you can do to make God love you less.

Love is the core of who God is, always and for ever. His love for you flows out of the essence of who he is and you are loved as you are right now. God doesn't love you more when you're on top of the world, when you achieve your goals or when you receive praise from people. God's love for you is settled and final. It never wavers. It is infinite, just as he is infinite. It's a force that never fails.

FOR FURTHER REFLECTION

Psalm 106:1
John 15:13

Lean on Him

When you lean on God you have a solid
rock that will never bend, waver, fade or crumble.
So place your whole weight on him.

Have you ever tried walking across a glass-bottomed bridge? The higher the bridge, the more daunting the experience. The usual initial reaction is one of caution as your foot reaches out for the first step, making sure there's a firm foundation. When there's confidence in the whole structure, walking across becomes much easier. Learning to lean your whole weight upon God is a similar process. It will take time to develop the confidence to completely transfer all your trust to him, but you will discover that the foundation you lean upon is a sure and steadfast rock that cannot be moved. Be assured that when you step out in faith, God has already got your next step on a secure platform.

FOR FURTHER REFLECTION

Proverbs 3:5

DAY 187

Let God Guide

*If you're going through a difficult time, ask God
to steer you through it. He is the captain of the ship
of life and will guide you through the storm.*

It's in the midst of the storm that dark clouds often obscure our vision. All we see are the swirling winds of strife that parade around our minds. Christ knows the path to take in every dark situation in our lives. 'Be not dismayed whate'er betide, God will take care of you; beneath his wings of love abide, God will take care of you' says the hymn by Civilla Martin. Let these words be your theme as you go through difficult times.

FOR FURTHER REFLECTION

Isaiah 30:21
Isaiah 58:11

Listen to God's Promptings

When you feel prompted to pray for someone, don't wait to do it! Your prayer could be what that person needs right at that moment in their present situation.

God answers petitions through the prayers of other people. This means that someone who is in desperate need may just need someone to pray for them on their behalf in that given moment. Intercessory prayer is a vital part our prayer life experience. It's not just about praying for yourself – when you are prompted, bring that person's name before God when you pray. You may not know what the full situation is, but that's not your concern. Just pray for that person – maybe you will see the answer to that prayer later on. The most important thing, however, is following up on the promptings.

FOR FURTHER REFLECTION

James 5:16

DAY 189

Keep Afloat

*Refuse to allow tomorrow's sea of
unknowns to flood into your reservoir today.
Otherwise you'll end up drowning!*

Trying to keep your head above water is not really a nice position to be in. It implies a constant battle to reach up for air. That's the position you get yourself in when you allow yourself to become overwhelmed, with too many things going on in your life. Taking on board both tomorrow's unknowns and today's issues will only engulf you. You have to separate the things you can control from the things you can't control. You don't want just to be gasping for air all the time – you need to stay afloat, on top of the situation!

FOR FURTHER REFLECTION

Matthew 6:25–33

Turn Around

*If you find you've wandered far away from God,
you only have to turn around. He's been behind
you all the time.*

When we turn away from God he does not stay still and wait for us to come back to him. He pursues us and sticks with us, not desiring that anyone should get lost. Like the shepherd who has a hundred sheep, when one goes missing, God does not stop searching until he finds that one sheep and brings it back home. So next time you feel distant from God, the likelihood is that it's you that has moved away. Just stop running, stand still and let God claim you back.

FOR FURTHER REFLECTION

Luke 15:4
Luke 19:10

Don't Wait Until It's Too Late

Flowers are meant to be sent to someone who can touch and smell them. Don't leave it until they cannot enjoy them.

Whether it's flowers or anything else that is a token of your love and appreciation, there's nothing like acting in the moment and letting someone know you care. How much money is often spent showering someone with gifts of kindness when they can't appreciate them, simply because you left it too late? Being mindful of someone who will benefit from your act of love ought to stimulate you into action, not procrastination.

FOR FURTHER REFLECTION

Galatians 6:9–10

Think Peaceful Thoughts

Agitation! Frustration! Complication! These words speak a sense of unrest. Calm, tranquillity, serenity – now don't those sound better?

Some of the very words we use can have an influence on our mood and demeanour. Our choice of negative or hostile words makes an association within the mind that reflects the meaning of the words we use. The same is true for words of calm and peace. Focusing on the words 'tranquillity' or 'serenity' draws your mind to scenes that depict those words, which in turn allows the body to respond in harmony. The saying is true: 'You are what you think!'

FOR FURTHER REFLECTION

Philippians 4:8
Proverbs 23:7

Don't Stay Down!

When you've been knocked flat on your back,
the only direction you can look is heavenwards.

God speaks to us in many different ways. However, we can become oblivious to God's promptings due to the many voices vying for our attention through social media, work demands and our own random thoughts. Sometimes the only way God can get through to us is through life's circumstances that knock us flat on our backs. It's when we are flat on our backs that the only way we can look is upwards. If we could save ourselves from that ordeal simply by taking time in the day to be still and listen to God, we would be in a much better position to face daily decisions.

FOR FURTHER REFLECTION

Psalm 145:14
Psalm 37:24

Live Joyfully

Happy people rarely spend time talking about happiness. They're too busy living it.

There are so many bestselling books today on how to be happy. The number of books sold implies how desperate people are to achieve this state of well-being. Indeed, it's almost instinctive to want to be happy, but what complicates things is the media's view of what constitutes happiness. People are given a picture of happiness achieved through material possessions, relationships, wealth and endless holidays. Yet happiness is simply your response to any given situation. When you can successfully appreciate moments with special people around you or even when alone, you begin to understand the source of happiness.

FOR FURTHER REFLECTION

Philippians 4:11
Proverbs 16:20

DAY 195

Face the Storm

Don't run away from your problem, face it!
Divide it into small parts and deal with each
one separately.

Problems can often appear bigger and larger than they really are. Fear and worry distort the true nature of the issue and it becomes amplified. If not kept in check it will snowball into something that becomes more overwhelming. Face your dilemma by writing down exactly what the problem is. That simple exercise alone will put things into perspective. Then dissect it into manageable parts – areas that you have control over and areas that you don't. That will tell you where to put your emphasis.

FOR FURTHER REFLECTION

Matthew 11:28–29
Psalm 55:22

Know Your Limits

Calm disappears when you try to do something about something you can't do anything about.

In every problem we encounter, there's always an element where there's absolutely nothing we can do ourselves to change or remedy the situation. The skill of problem-solving is knowing where your limits are. The moment you cross over into uncontrollable territory you amass a whole new level of problems for yourself. There are things God expects you to address with the wisdom he gives you, but there are also areas where he clearly says: 'To you this is off limits.' Don't cross over into 'God-only' territory!

FOR FURTHER REFLECTION

Matthew 19:26
Genesis 18:14

Listen to Calm

Soothing music is known to calm the soul.
Listen to something uplifting today and receive
a heart-warming experience.

Much like exercise, music has been shown to increase oxytocin levels in your brain, which can be an instant mood-booster. Oxytocin is also referred to as the 'love hormone', as it's associated with feelings of positive bonding, commitment, calmness and reduced anxiety. When music is combined with spiritual lyrics, there's an added bonus of calm and inspiration that uplifts the soul.

FOR FURTHER REFLECTION

1 Samuel 16:23

DAY 198

Look Beyond People's Opinion of You

*You would worry less about what people think of you
if you realised how seldom they do think of you.*

If you start paying less attention to what makes you *you* – your talents, beliefs and values –and conform to what others may or may not think, you'll harm your potential. You'll start playing it safe because you're afraid of what will happen on the other side of the critique. You'll fear being ridiculed or rejected. When challenged, you'll surrender your viewpoint. So stop trying to fit into false perceptions of people's view of you. Be confident in your own skin!

FOR FURTHER REFLECTION

Psalm 139:17–18

Develop an Attitude of Gratitude

It's surprising how just being grateful in your circumstances puts your life into perspective.

An attitude of gratitude means creating a conscious mindset to express thankfulness and being grateful for every aspect of your life regardless of your situation. When you have an attitude of gratitude you focus on expanding the positives in your life, rather than dwelling on the negatives. When you begin to express gratitude you feel more confident, positive and optimistic. You also feel happier and more joyful about the things you have and the people that matter most.

FOR FURTHER REFLECTION

1 Thessalonians 5:18

Don't Overwork

*If you make your work more important than yourself,
you won't be around to finish it!*

Overwork is a slow killer. If you're overdoing things, your levels of cortisol (the primary stress hormone) increase, leading to brain fog, high blood pressure and a host of other health problems. It's like driving a car on the red. Very soon the dregs and sludge clog up the engine, decreasing overall performance. The common side effects of overwork include insomnia, an imbalanced diet, little or no exercise and neglect of relationships. Ask yourself: 'Is it really worth it?'

FOR FURTHER REFLECTION

Proverbs 23:4–5
Matthew 6:19–21

Look Forward

With all the suffering we see today,
we look forward to the time when Christ returns.
God will 'wipe away every tear from our eyes;
there shall be no more death, nor sorrow, nor crying.
There shall be no more pain.'

We may carry certain sorrows throughout our journey of life. For a time there may be weeping all around us – it's one of the effects of living in a sinful world. But Jesus himself promises to wipe our tears away when he puts an end to everything associated with sin. When he does wipe away every tear, it will be for the last time. The new reality will be one with nothing to mourn because death will be no more. That's definitely something to fuel hope.

FOR FURTHER REFLECTION

Revelation 21:3–4
John 14:1–3

Be an Initiator

It's nice to be appreciated.

When you receive appreciation, pass it on to someone else. When was the last time you checked in with a friend or loved one to see how they're doing? If there's one thing the pandemic taught us, it's the value of our personal relationships and the importance of staying connected even while at a distance. Expressing appreciation is one of the best ways to strengthen your relationships. It doesn't take much to start off a chain reaction of expressing love, so why not let it start with you?

FOR FURTHER REFLECTION

Hebrews 13:1
John 15:12

Enjoy Your Day

*Today you will never know what you've been
protected from, but God knows. So enjoy your day –
God's watching over you!*

We are completely unaware of what goes in the spiritual world unseen to human eyes. The spiritual forces of good and evil are embarked in a daily conflict over our souls. Because we are treasured by God, the enemy of our souls seeks to sever that relationship and render us defeated. But with God on our side we cannot be defeated, so go through your day knowing that God has got you covered.

FOR FURTHER REFLECTION

2 Thessalonians 3:3
Psalm 103:4

Take a Break

Never feel guilty about taking a break. Jesus didn't –
he always found time to rest and recuperate.

Never taking a break from the tasks at hand actually reduces your ability to be creative. Your cognitive capacity is exhausted. But, taking a break will give you a fresh perspective on challenging projects. If you're skipping lunch to continue to push forward in a very intense project, then you're probably not doing yourself any favours. Giving yourself time to rest and recharge will energise you for the next task ahead. If Jesus recognised the need for this, then you know it's important.

FOR FURTHER REFLECTION

Mark 6:31

Learn from Children

*Bring out the child in you today. Go to the local park,
have fun and enjoy the surroundings – soon you'll
be giggling all over.*

Being an adult is pretty awesome, but it's also filled with lots of responsibilities and tough decisions. Slowly but surely, that child-like wonder you had as a kid is put in a box and tucked away in the attic of your brain. We put down our toys; we stop playing. We become more jaded, more structured and less open to new experiences. But as we grow into adulthood, we might be letting go of a little more than we should. Children jump, climb, fall and get right back up. The good news is that childlike wonder still lives inside you—no matter how old you are. It's just a matter of embracing it.

FOR FURTHER REFLECTION

Mark 10:15

Hold on for the Breakthrough

*It's when the burdens seem heaviest
that the breakthrough is near. Hold on for it!*

Don't give up when you have failed or sinned. Don't give up when your prayers have not yet been answered. Don't give up when the fragmenting effect of multiple pressures seems relentless. Don't give up when waiting for God seems endless. Look to Jesus, 'fight the good fight of faith' (1 Timothy 6:12), and if you get knocked down, get up and get back in the fight!

FOR FURTHER REFLECTION

Galatians 6:9

Put Your Faith into Action

When you can't figure it out,
you have to faith it out.

Jesus notices and responds when we express faith in him. Don't underestimate how important your faith is to him. Express it in every way you can. Act according to it all the time. Don't wait until you can't fathom it out. You have to do something to show God that you are serious about what you believe in. Know that Jesus delights in people who honour him, and when God sees your faith that's when extraordinary things will begin to happen.

FOR FURTHER REFLECTION

Mark 11:24
Hebrews 11:1

Control Your Thoughts

Think miserable thoughts and you will be miserable,
think fearful thoughts and you will be fearful,
think calming thoughts and you will be calm –
you become what you constantly think.

The mind is the combat zone. The Bible tells us to fix our thoughts on what is 'true, noble, just, pure, lovely and of good report'. Think about what you're thinking about. Ask yourself: 'Where did that thought come from?' If you can discipline yourself to examine what you're thinking about, you'll be in a better position to discern the origin of the thought.

FOR FURTHER REFLECTION

2 Corinthians 10:5
Proverbs 23:7
Philippians 4:8

Expect the Unexpected

Watch out for those surprising special moments –
an unexpected call from a friend, a compliment,
finding money in your coat from last winter.
Something pleasant often happens unexpectedly.

The game of treasure hunt goes down well especially with children. You see their eagerness as they scurry around the room, looking under chairs and in corners trying to find the hidden treasure. Because of their anticipation of finding something, they keep looking intently until at last it's discovered. Then you see broad smiles on their faces reflecting a sense of accomplishment. God delights in giving his children special gifts. Some are nestled away in secret places that can only be noticed when we eagerly look for them. Be assured that today something special is awaiting you – just look out for it!

FOR FURTHER REFLECTION

Isaiah 58:14
James 1:17

Follow the Light

There's a rainbow of hope and promise at the end of your storm. The sun will shine again.

Being in a dark tunnel can make you feel hopeless. However, it is a season that you must pass through. You will need determination and vision to walk through the tunnel. You must remind yourself that the light is indeed coming. When you get that first glimmer of light, know that it is a sign of improvement in a situation that has been going on for a long time. The light at the end of the tunnel is a long-awaited indication that a period of darkness is nearing an end.

FOR FURTHER REFLECTION

Matthew 10:39

Believe Yourself into Wellness

*One of the discoveries of modern medicine is
the more optimistic you are, the greater the chance of
maintaining health. Believe that you will get better –
you have nothing to lose!*

We all find ourselves coping with troubling thoughts from time to time, especially when we're going through changes in our lives or when we feel depressed, anxious, sad, angry or stressed out. Healthy thinking does not mean positive thinking! No one can look at things positively all the time. It's normal and healthy to feel upset and have negative thoughts when difficult things happen. Healthy thinking means looking at the entire situation – the positive, the negative and the neutral parts – and then coming to a conclusion. In other words, healthy thinking means looking at life and the world in a balanced way, not through rose-tinted glasses.

FOR FURTHER REFLECTION

John 20:31
Mark 11:24

Listen to Others

There's always someone worse off than you.
Take time to listen to other people's plights and
see how yours pales into insignificance.

If you are feeling low or in emotional pain, try to find someone you can talk to, someone who will listen deeply and without judgement. Talk to them about everything that's seriously bothering you. Not only will you feel better having vocalised an internal hurt or pain, but it allows you to put your situation into perspective. Moreover, when we also listen to what other people are going through we tend to reflect in that moment on our own situation. Sometimes the gravity of what you hear makes what you just shared more bearable in comparison.

FOR FURTHER REFLECTION

Galatians 6:2
Proverbs 14:21

Feel the Breeze

*Fresh air gives you sixty-six per cent of your energy.
Love the open air – it will re-energise you and
recharge you with zeal.*

Breathing in fresh air stimulates both the physical and the emotional being. It has the powerful capability to revitalise your emotions, even if you've had a bad day or week. We thrive off positive energy sources, and fresh air and sunlight are two of the most important forms of positive energy source. Fresh air helps you naturally wake up, so starting your morning with a walk can be a great way to begin the day. If you are trying to improve your health and well-being, go for a walk every day. The results are incomparable.

FOR FURTHER REFLECTION

3 John 2

Be Still

To hear God's voice clearly, get away from distractions and quiet your soul. Listen closely to his still, small voice.

Take a minute and meditate on this verse right now: 'Be still, and know that I am God.' This phrase is actually derived from the Hebrew word *rapha*, which means 'surrender in order that you may know'. Unlike those tangible realities in our everyday life that can be perceived simply by their existence, God's truth is that 'his strength is made perfect in weakness' (2 Corinthians 12.9). When we surrender ourselves, our lives, our wills and our desire, to him, he is more able to fully reveal himself to us and we are more able to fully experience him.

FOR FURTHER REFLECTION

Psalm 46:10
Isaiah 30:15

Put Yourself First

*A caring person often puts others before themselves.
There's no harm, however, in putting yourself first
for a change. A prerequisite to loving others is to
love yourself!*

In putting yourself first, you do what is in your best interest to enhance your personal, professional and spiritual life. Some may see this as being selfish – however, it is simply looking out for yourself so that you will be able to be of service and value to others. In taking care of yourself and putting yourself first you will find that you place yourself in a better position to help others. In loving and forgiving yourself, you are also able to remove blockages that have been stopping you from reaching your full potential. So go ahead and show yourself some love!

FOR FURTHER REFLECTION

Matthew 19:19
Mark 12:30–31

Get Calm, Get Peace

*A calm state of mind is naturally accompanied
by peace. Maintain calm and you maintain peace.*

The root of the Hebrew word for peace, *shalom*, means 'whole' and points to a two-fold meaning: peace within oneself and peace between people. Peace is an inner state of well-being and calm. As human beings, we allow many things to disturb our peace. There are four key emotions – fear, happiness, sadness and anger. Anything that activates your sadness, anger or fear has the potential to disturb your peace. Establishing a calm mind, however, overrides these threats and acts as a major defence mechanism against experiencing overwhelming negative emotions.

FOR FURTHER REFLECTION

John 14:27
Romans 15:13

Just Say It

Don't let self-centredness stop you from expressing love to the people in your life who need to hear it. Make that call, send those flowers, say: 'I love you.'

Telling somebody you love them feeds the relationship and keeps it alive. It reinforces your feelings and helps remind your loved ones – your spouse, sweetheart, child or parent – that you are there for them and that they matter to you. Saying 'I love you' and making other statements of affection are great ways to create that positive environment. Some people might feel a little awkward confessing their love, maybe because they might be wary of showing their vulnerabilities. What if your loved one doesn't say it back? That's what intimacy is – that I let you see all of me, knowing that you could reject me and abandon me, but hoping that you won't.

FOR FURTHER REFLECTION

1 Samuel 20:17

Trust More

The bottom line is, the more you trust God,
the more you lower your anxiety levels.

How do we surrender to God? First, tell him – it's a conscious choice that you need to make. Pray and acknowledge him as your Lord. Ask him to take over. Give him the key to your life. There is a hymn by Judson van der Venter that says: 'All to Jesus I surrender, humbly at his feet I bow; worldly pleasures all forsaken, take me, Jesus, take me now.' Most of us aren't really surrendering all. But this is what we need to be – fully surrendered to God. Surrender is an act of faith saying: 'Lord, I am trusting you.' Surrendering to God is not a once-and-for-all experience – this 'letting go and letting God' takes place on a daily basis. Each time you're confronted by an issue, a choice, a need, seek God and let him take over.

FOR FURTHER REFLECTION

Matthew 6:34
Psalm 22:24
1 Peter 5:6–7

Keep Your Cool

*Keeping your head when everything else is
losing theirs is an example of peace.*

Keeping a cool head is not easy these days. We have much
to be angry, sad and worried about, from economic concerns to
environmental threats. It is perfectly natural and normal to feel
these things in response to troubled times. Yet, these reactions
rarely do us any good. If left unchecked, our stress and negativity can undermine our health and threaten our relationships.
Remember, some problems take longer to get out of than others.
Be patient – break those problems down into smaller ones and
tackle them one at a time.

FOR FURTHER REFLECTION

Psalm 107:29–30
Galatians 5:22

Be Enthusiastic

Enthusiasm – what a wonderful action word!
It takes the sting out of challenging tasks and is
contagious, spreading rapidly to those around you.

Sometimes we find ourselves in an environment where our enthusiasm gets siphoned off. For example, if you are constantly in the company of negative people, you will take on a negative frame of mind. That's why you have to practise enthusiasm. You do that by thinking it, by believing it, by praying it, by talking it, until enthusiasm becomes part of your nature. Stop saying discouraging, hateful, negative and critical things. Think enthusiasm – talk it, live it, pray it, act it!

FOR FURTHER REFLECTION

Ecclesiastes 9:10

DAY 221

Think Calm

The very word 'calm' emits a sense of serenity and stillness. Meditate on the word and let it speak to you.

When you need to calm your mind and banish troubling thoughts, say this prayer:

Dear Lord, please come to my rescue, I'm in need of your help right now.
Turn me away from my tendency to block out or avoid my difficulties.
Release my mind from nagging thoughts and replace them with peaceful ones.
May your calming presence draw near to me,
that I may encounter your safety and protection.
I meditate on your goodness towards me.
Amen.

FOR FURTHER REFLECTION

Isaiah 26:3
Psalm 63:6

Avoid Unnecessary Stress

*More people today complain of insomnia, tension
headaches and panic attacks than ever before.
Avoid all this by daily accepting Christ's invitation:
'Come to me . . . and I will give you rest.'*

Rest is essential for us in many ways. Without rest our minds
and bodies are unable to function in the way they were designed
to. The same goes for the rest Jesus provides: without it we begin
to lean on ourselves and away from Jesus, driving our bodies and
minds alike to exhaustion. Resting in Jesus is something we are
called to tap into at all times. It is laying everything at his feet and
trusting that he will and has already done the work – all we need
to offer is our obedience.

FOR FURTHER REFLECTION

Matthew 11:28
Isaiah 40:30–31

Value Loved Ones

*There are special people God has placed in your
life for a reason. It may be for a season or longer,
but acknowledge, appreciate and treasure them.*

The more closely we are connected to the people we love, the happier we feel and the more personal satisfaction we have in our lives. These moments of connection and shared enjoyment with loved ones are the most important life experiences. Forming connections that make up our identity contributes to our well-being. It is from the web of our relationships and connections with work colleagues, neighbours and significant others that we draw our strength. Such people can lift us when we are down and give us the capacity to deal with whatever challenges come our way.

FOR FURTHER REFLECTION

Ecclesiastes 4:9–10
Proverbs 17:17

Avoid a 'Must Do' Mentality

*What limits calm? A sense of 'must do' or obligation,
and the unending list of things ahead that simply
have to be done!*

We will find that once we deplete ourselves through overwork, we have less energy and focus to help us resist temptations, be kind to others or engage in spiritual practices. In an unfocused state of mind, we are likely to say and do things that go against our principles. We lose our temper, miss important family commitments and fail to notice the needs of others. Break out of this downward spiral – never allow a sense of obligation to control and dictate your behaviour. Take stock, pause, reflect and assess your situation with a clear mind. God has promised that if we focus on him he will keep our minds in perfect peace.

FOR FURTHER REFLECTION

**Isaiah 26:3
Ecclesiastes 3:1–9**

Believe God's Truth

Sometimes we suffer more in thoughts than in reality.
Bring your thoughts in line with the truth!

It's normal to have negative thoughts, no matter how extreme they might be at times. The issues arise when we believe our thoughts are true and in our minds they turn into a worst-case scenario that makes us feel even more anxious. Don't let these thoughts dictate your sense of well-being – imagine placing each negative thought in your mind on a leaf and watch the leaf float down a stream. When you have another thought, as you will, put it on another leaf and watch the leaf float away.

FOR FURTHER REFLECTION

Psalm 117:2
James 3:14

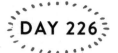
Treat Yourself

Learn to live with yourself by enjoying your own company. Let yourself know you're worth a treat!

Treating yourself may sound like a self-indulgent, frivolous strategy, but it's not. When the demands of life become overwhelming, treats play an important role. When we give ourselves treats, we feel energised, cared for and content, which boosts our self-esteem. This boost helps us maintain our sense of well-being. So go ahead and treat yourself today – go for a massage or spa treatment, have a relaxing bath or just curl up with your favourite book.

FOR FURTHER REFLECTION

Psalm 62:5

Live at Ease

*There is calmness when life is lived in
gratitude and quiet joy.*

In the hustle and bustle of daily life, sometimes it's all too easy
to block out the details of the day, forgetting that each and every
day holds precious gifts. From the air we breathe to the friendships we hold dear, there is *always* something to be thankful for.
Gratitude is a special gift given to us by God. It is about not
taking things for granted, but being thankful for what we have
and receive. Thankfulness is a powerful means of drawing near
to God.

FOR FURTHER REFLECTION

Psalm 107:29–30

Fear Not

*Surprisingly often, the things we fear the
most never come to pass.*

Fear is seldom based on truth. It's based on false expectations and assumptions about events that are very unlikely to occur, as the acrostic below cleverly points out.

False

Expectations

Appearing

Real

More importantly, fear forgets that God is God. He is still in control!

FOR FURTHER REFLECTION

Deuteronomy 1:21
Psalm 118:6–7

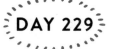

Care for Yourself

Look after yourself. There is only one you!

We all want to be healthy and enjoy a long, happy life. But we may not realise that each of us holds the answer to achieving these things within ourselves. It's called self-care, which is the thoughtful practice of protecting and improving our own physical and mental health within a balanced lifestyle. In these stressful and uncertain times, it's never been more critical. Self-care includes the intentional acts of eating well, getting enough sleep, exercising regularly, maintaining a strong social network, tending to our spiritual needs and so much more. Think of it as the gentle art of loving yourself.

FOR FURTHER REFLECTION

Ephesians 2:10
1 Corinthians 3:16

Use Your Past for Good

The moment you accept God's
forgiveness you no longer have a dark past.
You have a bright future!

Though our mistakes may keep us humble, it's also easy to be down on ourselves because of them. Sometimes we dwell on mistakes we've made, even years later. While we cannot change the things we have done in the past, we can use them to learn how to move forward. Each mistake and every lesson we learn helps us develop into even better versions of ourselves. Now that we understand that no one is perfect and mistakes are a universal part of everyone's personal growth, we are better able to understand when someone *else* makes a mistake. Our past mistakes can help us to empathise with another's journey and to offer advice based on what we have learned from our own trials.

FOR FURTHER REFLECTION

Philippians 3:13
Psalm 51

Write It Down

*Keeping a journal is an excellent way to
capture and treasure those special moments
that could easily be forgotten otherwise.*

Keeping a journal to look back on is probably one of the most rewarding daily tasks. Your memories can also serve as a record of your thoughts for posterity. Keeping a journal is an opportunity to leave a unique legacy – your mind transposed onto paper. You are writing in your journal for just you and God, so do not be afraid to put it all in there. God knows your heart and what you truly want, so it is time to come to terms with it yourself and be honest. By reading your own journal's record of God's providence in the past, you can be emboldened to believe that he will yet again be faithful to you in the future.

FOR FURTHER REFLECTION

Revelation 1:19
Jeremiah 30:2

Hug Someone

*Hugging is healing. It generates a spirit of calm
and well-being for the hugger and the hugged alike.*

There are significant health benefits from hugging. Stress reduction, a boosted immune system, a lower risk of heart disease and less depression can all result from a 10-second hug a day. Try increasing your hug awareness with your sweetheart, children, parents or friends. If you feel like you aren't a hugger, see what happens if you just reach out and touch, hold hands, or put your arm around your loved ones a little more often. Make it an experiment and explore how increased touch impacts your relationships and your mood.

FOR FURTHER REFLECTION

Song of Solomon 8:3
Acts 20:37

Depend on God

Becoming a Christian is the work of a moment.
Learning to depend on God is the work of a lifetime.
You're still a work in progress.

The difficulty arises when you have to depend on God because you're not in complete control of the issues you face. But take stock of what you're already doing – you already depend on God for many things. Just the mere fact that you're alive today is a testimony that you can depend on God. You depend on him to give you the breath of life to see another day, to give you the strength to go to work and for protection. When you learn to depend on God for everything, what you're really doing is releasing control of your life and handing the steering wheel over to him. It will take time, but you will get there.

Ecclesiastes 7:8
Philippians 4:6
James 5:8

Let God Mould You

Someone who is content says: 'I am who I am.
I cannot be anyone other than who God has called
me to be. I will be the best version of me and will
accept each day and what it brings.'

God wants us to understand that he lovingly made us, and he wants us to accept the way he made us. When you become a disciple, God the potter doesn't change who you are. He doesn't change your personality – he simply uses who you are to better effect. Self-acceptance is the key to usefulness for God. You can ask the potter who formed you what he has in mind for you. Accept how he made you, and then step back and let him transform you.

FOR FURTHER REFLECTION

Isaiah 64:1–9
John 3:27

Watch Your Mood

Many ailments are of emotional origin.
Back pain, palpitations and ulcers can all be linked
to negative emotions. Next time you feel discomfort,
check your mood.

If feelings of stress, sadness or anxiety are causing you physical problems, keeping these feelings inside can make you feel worse. Focus on the things that you are grateful for in your life. Try not to overthink the problems at work, school or home that lead to negative feelings. This doesn't mean you have to pretend to be happy when you feel stressed, anxious or upset. It's important, however, to deal with negative feelings – but try to focus on the positive things in your life too. Remember, your body responds to the way you think, feel and act!

FOR FURTHER REFLECTION

Psalm 25:18
Job 15:20

Let God Guide

Since God is 'the same yesterday, today and forever', we can take the God of yesterday, walk with him today and ask him for guidance for tomorrow.

We serve a God who is consistent. That doesn't mean he is predictable, it simply means he is completely and totally dependable. It's because of God's unwavering trustworthiness that you can be assured he's always going to turn up for you. There's no better person in your life right now than the one who is faithful and consistently present to guide you in all your ways. Trust him with your life and with your future!

FOR FURTHER REFLECTION

Hebrews 13:8
Psalm 139:7

Let God Read It

*What is the prayer of your heart? Write it down
on a piece of paper, then spread it out before God.*

Try writing out what's on your heart right now. What's worrying you? What's causing you concern or frustration? Write it out on paper. The act itself is quite soothing as you transfer your thoughts to the paper. Now comes the best part – spread out the paper before God. Lay it down as you kneel in prayer and present it before God.

FOR FURTHER REFLECTION

2 Kings 19:14–37

Stay Hopeful

Every new morning brings a new message of hope.
They appear in many ways – identify them.

Would you believe that we probably only notice two per cent of all of God's blessings each day? It's because we focus on so many other things that God's blessings come and pass us by. Sometimes we receive them but can't identify them as a blessing. So be assured that when you awake each morning, there are a myriad of opportunities to reinforce your trust and faith in God – blessings abound in multiple ways moment by moment, and new messages of hope are all vying for your attention. Ask God to open your eyes to see them.

FOR FURTHER REFLECTION

James 1:17–18
2 Corinthians 9:8–10

Don't Waste Your Money

A joyful way of life is something money cannot buy.
Experience contentment through cheap and
cheerful things.

The challenge for us is to learn to be almost subconsciously grateful. Think of a sunny day, blue water, flowers in a vase, leaves turning red, the sunrise and sunset, when the day breaks and even at twilight. Feel gratitude as naturally as you breathe, without even thinking. That's what having an attitude of gratitude means. When your whole outlook towards life is just one great big feeling of gratitude, then you have arrived.

FOR FURTHER REFLECTION

1 Thessalonians 5:18
Psalm 118:24

Be Inspired

*Play spiritual music to soothe your soul
while you work, drive, clean, cook or relax.
The harmonious sound can be inspiring.*

Music has significant effects on our mind and body, such as elevating our mood and decreasing pain and anxiety. It triggers the release of happy hormones, stimulates the immune system, improves focus and influences heart rate and breathing. By listening to music you can even strengthen the emotional and cognitive centres of the brain. That is why music is one of the most effective ways to deal with mood disorders. So whenever you feel low or have a rough day at work, play some soft, soothing music to elevate your mood.

FOR FURTHER REFLECTION

Colossians 3:16
Psalm 95:1–2

Take Charge

*When you are in the middle of chaos,
be assured it will pass away. So relax, breathe
and maintain a positive outlook.*

Trouble does not last for ever. You may be perplexed, not knowing what to do, especially since everything you have tried has not worked out, but you don't have to be in despair. You may be persecuted, talked about, lied about, but you are never forsaken. You are not alone. God will never forsake you and he will not allow you to be destroyed. Yes, even those who love the Lord go through trials, tribulation and trouble, but trouble doesn't last for ever.

FOR FURTHER REFLECTION

2 Corinthians 4:8–18

Reflect

*Take a few moments to contemplate
something you are especially grateful for.*

There is so much that is wrong with the society we live in. There is so much about ourselves that we wish to change. In an attempt to make ourselves better and to change our society, often we forget to be grateful for the things we do have. We focus so much on the negative that the positive loses its place in our hearts. No matter how you think of it, life is a gift. So many individuals don't get a chance to make it as far as you did. Disease, poverty, famine and drought claim thousands of lives each year, but you get to live, to survive, to exist and to be able to dream. Be grateful for your life.

FOR FURTHER REFLECTION

1 Thessalonians 5:18
Colossians 3:17

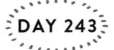

Appreciate the Little Things

Before you go to sleep make a list of
five little things that made you happy today.
Then say a prayer of thanksgiving for them.

Happiness is found in the simplest things. When life just gets to you, take a step back and think of all the things that make you happy. It will counteract a bad day. Write down a few things every day that makes you happy – a sunny spring day, clean laundry, cosy blankets, a good book, looking at pictures from your summer holiday – you'll be surprised at the simple things in life that can put a smile on your face!

FOR FURTHER REFLECTION

1 Thessalonians 5:16–18

Count Your Joys

Retrain your mind not to focus on the one bad thing, but rather on the nine good things.

Your thoughts or feelings have a way of lifting you up or dragging you down. We have all experienced emotional mountain-top experiences and, sadly, you may have also experienced times of despair. As believers, we can be positive at times, and other times we might become negative if we are not careful. When we focus on the negative it can be very difficult to see the positive. As the sayings go: 'You are what you eat', 'Garbage in, garbage out' and 'What you focus on is how you will think.' Focus on what is excellent and praiseworthy and let your actions follow suit.

FOR FURTHER REFLECTION

Ephesians 1:3
Psalm 118:1–18

Calm Your Anger

When you're angry, try this meditation:
Breathing in, I calm my anger.
Breathing out, I take care of my anger.

We all get angry at times. Sometimes anger causes us to develop feelings of vengeance or hatred. The problem comes when we act on those negative feelings which can be destructive. We need to be in touch with our feelings and take responsibility for them. A person who rules their spirit demonstrates self-control. This means when you feel anger rising, you can choose not to act on it if you know it's against the Word of God.

FOR FURTHER REFLECTION

Proverbs 16:32
Ephesians 4:26–27

Question Yourself

Ask yourself: 'What am I waiting for to make me happy? Why am I not happy right now?'

Regardless of what is going on around you, you can feel happier, be productive, attract success and enjoy yourself. Happiness can only be experienced in the present, in the moment of whatever it is that you are trying to achieve right now. Whether you're at home cleaning out the garage, making a sandwich, hoovering the house or doing the gardening, it is your right to enjoy yourself.

FOR FURTHER REFLECTION

Philippians 4:4

Give with a Willing Heart

Remember that being generous is a blessing.

Research has shown that generous people have more fulfilling relationships. The research revealed that:

1. People always prefer the company of a generous giver to the company of a selfish hoarder.

2. People are naturally attracted to those who have an open heart to share with others.

3. Those who are generous also tend to value what they own. People who donate money are far less wasteful with the money left over.

4. People who give their time make better use of their remaining time.

The points above may be nothing new, but serve as an encouraging reminder.

FOR FURTHER REFLECTION

2 Corinthians 9:7

Nip It in the Bud

The sooner we openly recognise and acknowledge strife and stop feeding the fire, the sooner it will burn out.

The concept of adding fuel to the fire becomes real during times of conflict or strife. Many forms of legal dispute between two people occur when things escalate to a point of no return. Pride sets in and neither party is prepared to listen or compromise in any way. As a result, tens of thousands of pounds are spent in legal fees. When you sense issues arising, putting them off or minimising the situation is a slippery slope towards further complications and headaches. Identify the growing shoots of a problem and decide if it's really worth the battle.

FOR FURTHER REFLECTION

Matthew 18:15–17

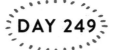

Discover Your Priority

*What changes do you need to make in your life
to have a closer walk with God? Whatever they are,
make them the main focus for change in your life.*

What does making God a priority look like? For a start, beginning the day with him in prayer, then making time for regular devotion, including him in your goals and plans for the future, finding a day in the week when you can spend time in worship and guarding these special moments so that other things don't take away from your time with God. It's when you decide to make God a priority in your life that you will find he takes care of all your other priorities. It's being intentional about how you protect your time so that it doesn't impinge on what's spiritually important.

FOR FURTHER REFLECTION

Matthew 6:33

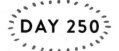

Walk by Faith

*You must still believe when there is no sign.
Just because you don't see something happening
on the outside, doesn't mean something is not
happening on the inside.*

Society almost demands that seeing is believing. To some extent it is, but in the spiritual realm, where faith becomes an important factor, not everything is revealed to us. God in his wisdom knows when to reveal his handiwork from the domain of the spiritual to that which our physical eyes can behold. The true test of faith, however, is learning to walk by faith, not by sight. This means taking God at his word – believing in his promises and trusting him in the process of waiting. So, keep on the path of faith, ask God to develop within you the 'inner sight' to see by faith what has yet to be revealed to human eyes.

FOR FURTHER REFLECTION

2 Corinthians 5:7
2 Kings 6:17–20

Zoom Out

Shift your perspective.
There is so much more in the picture.

The pandemic has certainly brought a new set of vocabulary that has stuck with us. Zoom meetings have become a true legacy of lockdown. But there are also times when we have to zoom out mentally. Sometimes our problems are all we can see; the hard thing right in front of us can take up our whole view and head space. We become so absorbed with the issue before us that we can't see what's around it. All we see is the big mountain before us and our failure to see a path that leads around or through it. If you can zoom out, you will begin to see the bigger picture and gain some context for your situation. You can approach it with more engagement and hope.

FOR FURTHER REFLECTION

2 Kings 6:14–17

Be Honest

Admit that you do not know all the answers.
Just say: 'I don't know.'

Many people will claim to be honest with themselves, but deep down they are not. In fact some won't even know that they are not and will continue to experience negativity in their lives. If you find yourself shifting blame onto others all the time, the chances are that you are suffering from self-deception. You are too blind to see fault in yourself, not because it doesn't exist, but because you have put a barrier in front of the problems. Be who you are and say what you feel – those who matter won't mind, and those who mind don't matter. Simply put, honesty begins with you and not the people around you.

FOR FURTHER REFLECTION

Psalm 51:6
John 8:32

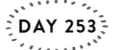

Let It Go

Let go of regret. Why relive something that
went wrong? Wasn't it bad enough the first time?

Letting go helps us to face the reality that we don't control life. The only aspect we do control is our attitude. Sometimes losing one thing opens you up to something else. It might be a lesson that helps you be more effective and happier in the future, or it could be a new possibility you never even thought of seeking. Maybe it won't benefit you in any discernible way right now. However, choosing to live with regrets is perhaps the most debilitating choice you can make. But the way to get over regret is not to ignore it. It's to push through it. It's to engage with your former self, to talk to yourself directly and understand why you did what you did. We need to sympathise with our former selves, to care for them, and ultimately, to forgive them.

FOR FURTHER REFLECTION

1 Peter 5:7
1 John 1:9

Check the Mirror

Your expression is the most important thing you wear.
Yet all expressions stem from how we feel inside.
It's hard to fake your facial expression if inside you
feel something different from what you are trying
to portray.

Our outward appearance is important, but it doesn't matter how pretty or handsome a person is on the outside. If they are selfish, greedy, unkind or dishonest they are not beautiful. It's a terrible burden to be attractive on the outside, but to lack the inner beauty which comes from faith in God. Focus on your inner self-worth. Work on your attitudes towards life and other people. When you have inner joy, peace and love reigning in your heart, your facial expression over time will not be able to contradict it.

FOR FURTHER REFLECTION

1 Peter 3:3–4
Proverbs 31:30

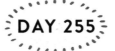

Pay Attention to Yourself

Listen to your thoughts – they become your actions.
Watch your actions – they become your habits.

The Bible often speaks about the power of the mind and our thoughts. Our minds are powerful and our thoughts shape who we are and will become. Changing the way you think changes your perspective, which changes how you act in the world. Jesus challenged people to change their thinking, because however many times you hear the words of God, if your mind (which symbolises the heart) doesn't change, there will be no conversion. That's why Christ said that we have to experience a change in the heart first, which will then be manifested in how we live and interact. Christ often challenged the religious leaders for focusing on their outward appearance. If you want real change, it's got to start in your heart. There has to be a real conversion experience.

FOR FURTHER REFLECTION

Romans 12:2

Learn from Others

*Close your eyes and picture the most loving
and compassionate individuals you have ever known
or heard about. Then think what you can learn
from them.*

We can't underestimate the importance of learning from the people around us. When we're open to learning from others, we benefit from their experiences and we can inherit their wisdom and knowledge. Learning from others is not a passive process, but one that requires work and commitment on our part. It involves listening to their stories and the life lessons they learned. Adapting their lessons to your situation makes the full cycle complete. You don't have to repeat the mistakes of others to learn the same lessons, and you can quickly adopt gems of wisdom from their life experiences.

FOR FURTHER REFLECTION

Philippians 4:9
Philippians 3:17

Begin the Change

*Don't be angry at yourself for feeling angry,
or guilty for feeling guilty. Simply recognise and
acknowledge your negative feelings – it is the
first step toward changing them.*

Because we have tens of thousands of thoughts a day, it is impossible to monitor each one. But an easy way to identify your predominant thoughts is to tune into your feelings, because your feelings are the result of your thoughts. Don't feel guilty or afraid because you are experiencing a negative emotion or thinking a negative thought, as that is just adding more negativity! Self-awareness is the key. Once you are aware of why you are feeling a particular way, you can then understand what your emotions are telling you and what changes you can make to improve your circumstances.

FOR FURTHER REFLECTION

Isaiah 26:3

Disappointed?
Get Reappointed

When one door closes, trust God to open another
one – it will calm your thoughts and emotions.

Even though we will experience disappointments in life, we can always get 'reappointed'. If you have a doctor's appointment and there's an emergency which leads to a cancellation, you simply make another appointment. Life can be that way too. Trusting that God has a good plan for you and that your steps are ordered by him is the key to preventing disappointment from turning into despair. How do you react when you get disappointed? Trust God completely and believe that his plan for you is infinitely better than your own plan.

FOR FURTHER REFLECTION

Proverbs 20:24

Settle Yourself Down

The quieter you are, the more you can hear.

You need to be honest about the real cause of your stress or anxiety. Is it your circumstances in life, or is it the way you respond to the circumstances? What complicates things the most is when we fail to be still to hear the voice of God. We need to learn to be still and rest physically, mentally, emotionally and spiritually. Entering the rest of God should be our number one priority if we are to hear his voice clearly. We may say that we are trusting God, but there is no evidence of trust unless we take time to sit quietly in the presence of God.

FOR FURTHER REFLECTION

Hebrews 4:10

Engage in Replacement Therapy

Confront a negative emotion with a positive one.

If you intend to enjoy the best life God has for you, then you must realise that the change you are waiting for begins in you. You must believe what God's Word says about you more than you believe what others say or what your own feelings tell you. Your circumstances are not your problem, because they won't last, but until you change your thinking, no matter what's going on in your life, you will still be stuck. See yourself as God sees you, not the way the world sees you or even the way you see yourself. Decide to believe the truth, then replace all negativity with the positive attributes that come from serving God. The circumstances may remain the same, but we change the glass we look through.

FOR FURTHER REFLECTION

Isaiah 61:3

Control Yourself

Know when to exercise restraint.
It gives you control over your life.

Self-control can be a powerful tool in the hands of a determined, disciplined individual. It can help you confront any problem and adjust your lifestyle. However, not everyone is able to exercise this control of the self in certain situations. The greatest temptations arise when the enemy, who knows our weaknesses, presents us with a situation where the likelihood is that we will succumb. These temptations can range from overindulgence in your favourite food to loss of temper, sexual immorality or overspending. Self-control is a fruit of the Spirit – invite the Spirit of God into your life today and let him develop this fruit in your life.

FOR FURTHER REFLECTION

Galatians 5:22–23
2 Peter 1:5–6

Be Your Own Boss

Talk yourself into relaxing.
Say to yourself: 'I give you permission to relax.'

You are the steward of your own body. See your life as a gift from God who entrusts you to take good care of it. That means giving your body nutritious food, good rest, exercise and spiritual nourishment. When you overindulge in anything it takes its toll on the body. You may not see the effects instantaneously, but over time constant abuse of the body will manifest itself. So look after yourself! Treat your body well. Take time to actually listen to what your body needs. If you don't, it will express its concerns in other ways such as through headaches, abscesses, fatigue or disease. When you show respect to your body, it will respond accordingly. You are the boss, and when you find yourself having overworked or neglected yourself in any way, do yourself a favour and relax. The rest will recharge you to do your next task with greater effectiveness.

FOR FURTHER REFLECTION

1 Corinthians 6:19–20

Enjoy Life!

God has a wonderful sense of humour – he made the long-necked giraffe, the cheeky monkey and the laughing hyena. Be assured, he wants you to see the bright side of life.

From the very beginning, we were created in God's image. What an immense honour it is to have the features of God, to be like him. If we have a sense of humour, then the one who created us has a sense of humour too. God reveals his sense of humour through the animals he created: the ostrich, the elephant seal, the platypus, the kangaroo and many others. He first surrounded Adam with these creatures to relieve Adam's loneliness, and one way of doing this was by making Adam laugh! There's too much strife and hardship in the world to go around each day with long faces. Even though we hear bad news every day, it's good to take stock of our lives and what God has blessed us with. Use your God-given sense of humour to really get the most out of life.

FOR FURTHER REFLECTION

Psalm 37:4
Ecclesiastes 3:4

Hold Your Tongue

Refrain from gossip, deceit, slander and harmful speech. Such things are only damaging and destructive.

The one member of our body that gets us into more trouble than anything else is our tongue. An untamed tongue can result in people losing all hope, becoming emotionally scarred, having their reputations ruined and losing friends for ever. So let us allow the Holy Spirit to tame and guide our tongue, so that our words will be uplifting, encouraging and glorifying to God. It takes time to tame anything, but the tongue can be reckless if it's not under control. We know that ultimately the words we speak come from the heart. So guard your lips every time you feel you are about to say something that is dishonest or will not glorify God.

FOR FURTHER REFLECTION

Psalm 34:13
James 3:5–8

Check Your Triggers

*Let go of the 'I've got to . . .', 'I need to . . .',
'I have to . . .', 'I want to . . .' feelings that can lie
at the heart of what we do.*

The demands of life can be taxing. There seems to be a never-ending list of things to do. Prioritising your time helps you to work out what is important and weed out the tasks that can wait for another day. Having a 'must do now' mentality will only rob you of vital energy and strength. Managing your time is about doing the urgent and important things first. Categorising your to-do list honestly is a starting point and will help you to avoid running yourself ragged. So re-evaluate what spurs you on – if there's an anxious need to try to cram everything in, then your tasks will not be performed adequately. To use time effectively, we have to learn how to be structured and disciplined. Plan your day wisely, and always factor in time to refresh yourself.

FOR FURTHER REFLECTION

Ephesians 5:15–17
Colossians 4:5

Treasure Quiet Moments

Delight in having time alone.
Don't call it loneliness; call it 'aloneness' or solitude.

Finding quiet time is something you have to be proactive about. It's not just being alone, for there are still many things that can preoccupy your mind. It's about switching off and not allowing your mind to run riot with all sorts of issues and problems. Calming your mind involves feeding it on that which brings it into a state of relaxation. This could be meditating, tuning into the natural world around you or listening to soothing music. In the business of life such moments can be rare, so make the best of them and appreciate every moment.

FOR FURTHER REFLECTION

Mark 1:35
Psalm 62:1

Aim High

Hope for the best, aim for the best,
but be perfectly content with whatever comes.

God wants us to be successful in all that we do. His idea of success is when we achieve our best in whatever sphere of life we are in, but alongside that, we are also endeavouring to live a life according to his will. The two are entwined – if we achieve great things in the world without having God alongside us we have not been successful. On the other hand, if we don't achieve what we desired, but have still maintained a connected relationship with God, we have been successful. So yes, aim high, strive to do your best, get the best grades you can and move up the ranks in your vocation, but never leave God out of the equation.

FOR FURTHER REFLECTION

Proverbs 16:3
1 Kings 2:3

DAY 268

Learn from Mistakes

Don't let past mistakes get you down – you can always learn from them. If God is patient with you, then be patient with yourself.

Aren't you glad God does not treat us the way we treat ourselves? We can be so hard and unforgiving towards ourselves when we've messed up. We take a long time to process and work through things and even condemn ourselves for our weaknesses and failures. God sees us in a different way. He already knows we are susceptible in many areas of life, but he factors all this into his decision to love us unconditionally anyhow. So embrace God's patience towards you when you fall – he will always be there for you. He's not going to leave you!

FOR FURTHER REFLECTION

Isaiah 41:10
Philippians 3:13

Stay Strong in Weakness

When your faith becomes weak, don't despair.
The apostle Paul said: 'When I am weak, then I am strong.'
Let God fight your battles!

We can't be strong all the time. In fact, we reveal our weaknesses every day. Contrary to popular opinion, weakness is not a sign of lack of power – in the spiritual realm it is a requirement for power. It's when we acknowledge our weakness that we are in a position to reach out for the strength that comes from God. Furthermore, our weaknesses make us qualified for the Holy Spirit to work in us, as the Spirit's work can really only be effective when all self is removed. So be assured – if you're feeling weak today, resources are on their way to help you get through.

FOR FURTHER REFLECTION

2 Corinthians 12:10
Nehemiah 8:10

Don't Be Fooled

*Wisdom replaces ignorance when you realise
that happiness does not lie in the accumulation of
more and more material things.*

Covetousness is a sneaky thing. It makes you want more and more. It makes you jealous of what other people around you have. It makes you miss out on opportunities to spend time with your family by working long hours to be able to buy the things you desire so desperately. God gives material blessings to us so that we can be a blessing to others, not to maintain a luxurious lifestyle to benefit our greed. Life is not about the here and now, but about eternity. We can't take our things with us into Heaven, but we can definitely use them to benefit others while we are still living on earth. So let wisdom prevail – when God blesses you with things in life, know that happiness lies in being grateful to the one who gave you what you have.

FOR FURTHER REFLECTION

Matthew 6:19–21

Love the Dawn

Give thanks for the morning light,
for your life and for your strength.

It's so simple – if you're wondering what to give God thanks for, then start with the basics! As you wake up, look round you. What do you see? The morning light. What do you hear? The sounds of life around you. Each new day is an opportunity to acknowledge the simple things that we often take for granted in life. Never assume that the morning light will come – when we awake in the morning, it's a gift of life from the Creator. With this gift, each new day comes with wonderful opportunities to learn something new, to become a blessing to someone or to be the recipient of something God has in store for you. So embrace the new day, be grateful for life and know that someone's life may be enriched by something you say or do and you may never know about it. Embrace the possibilities of a new day!

FOR FURTHER REFLECTION

Lamentations 3:22–24
Psalm 118:24

Accept Yourself, Accept Others

*Make friends with yourself by accepting who
you fully are. This will ultimately lead you towards
accepting other people.*

Contrary to what many believe, self-love is healthy. It's neither selfish nor self-indulgent. Most people think too little of themselves and often being in love is merely a compensation for inner emptiness, loneliness and shame. But as the Bible says 'Love your neighbour as yourself', how can loving your neighbour be a virtue and self-love be a vice? You're part of humanity, as worthy of love as the next person. Many people seek to love others, but are unable to love themselves. They believe that having a high regard for themselves is indulgent, conceited, arrogant or selfish. The opposite is true. The greater your love of self, the greater will be your love of others. You will be able to offer someone else your attention, respect, support, compassion and acceptance. As you develop these abilities, your capacity to love yourself and others grows.

FOR FURTHER REFLECTION

Mark 12:31
Psalm 139:14

Take Comfort

The name given to Jesus at birth, 'Immanuel –
God with us!', expresses the intent and purpose of
Christ's mission even today. Be assured that by
virtue of his name you are never alone!

Jesus never actually bore the name Immanuel during his earthly life. The name indicates his role, bringing God's presence to man. The phrase 'God with us' describes the nature of Jesus. He is God who became man. When Jesus was born, God came down and dwelt among us. Another way we might think about this language of 'God with us' is that Jesus offers us friendship. Jesus is not only with us as a saviour from our sins and as our strength when we are weak, but he's with us as a friend. He comes to us and holds out not only his strong arm to defend us but his hand in fellowship.

FOR FURTHER REFLECTION

Matthew 1:23
John 1:1–18

Listen First

Try to listen without interrupting,
judging or assuming what is being said.

Communication is really all about listening and understanding. We may be eloquent in speech, or have the best way of expressing ourselves, but if we can't listen effectively to the other person, the cycle of communication has not taken place. Simple skills in listening result in a reflective response to what has been said. We have a lot of good talkers today, but there is a dearth of good listeners – people who will give you their undivided time and attention. Maybe there's someone in your life who just needs to be listened to, without you giving them your advice, guidance or opinion. Be a listening ear to someone today!

FOR FURTHER REFLECTION

James 1:19
Psalm 34:15

Be Saved to Save

Use common sense.
Put on your oxygen mask first, then help others.

This is an important metaphor for those who spend a great deal of their time helping others. Taking care of others can easily deplete you if you don't take care of yourself. You can experience burnout, stress, fatigue, reduced mental effectiveness, health problems, anxiety, frustration and inability to sleep. Are you experiencing any of these symptoms? Caregivers need to replenish their energy and reserves in order to continue to take care of others. So put on your oxygen mask on first. It's time to let go of the guilt and take care of yourself.

FOR FURTHER REFLECTION

Philippians 4:13
Mark 6:31

You Are Valuable

Remind yourself this morning of your intrinsic value by saying aloud: 'I am deeply loved, cherished and highly thought of by my creator.'

Worldly self-esteem bases your worth on appearance, possessions and accomplishments. Whether high or low, this kind of self-image is proud, focuses on self and doesn't add value to your life. It minimises your potential for growth and influence. On the other hand, a self-image based upon the value God has placed on you is Christ-centred – God values you far more than you can dream or imagine. You are valuable because of who you are, made in God's image. You are valuable because of what you cost. We came at a high price, the death of his Son. You are valuable because of what you can become. As a person who is loved by God and adopted into his family, you can be sure that God has a plan for your life.

FOR FURTHER REFLECTION

Isaiah 66:2
Ephesians 4:1–4

Claim Your Heritage

As long as you adopt a diminished sense of self-worth, you will keep attracting the wrong people. Remember you are highly valued, an heir of the Kingdom and the child of the heavenly King!

You are royalty. This can be easy to forget in the busy and mundane moments of life, but the reality remains the same; because of Jesus, you're royalty! Not only this, but you were designed to reign in every area of life. Through the blood of Jesus, you are righteous, holy, chosen, spotless, blameless, royal, and you have been blessed with every spiritual blessing. Let that sink in for a minute.

FOR FURTHER REFLECTION

Revelation 5:10
1 John 3:1–2

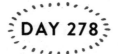

Live for Today

Too often we live in the past, recounting all the problems we've had to deal with. You can't change the past, but you can experience the joys and opportunities of today.

Coping with a painful past can include hiding ourselves behind a facade of endless activity. We can try to cover our pain by eliminating any time to think, rest or be refreshed. But sticking plasters don't bring inner healing. They only cover the scars or open wounds. Accepting the truth that God has already covered your past will help eliminate your own painful coping methods. But it means trusting God daily with the details of your life. He will bless your todays and reinforce your tomorrows if you live in anticipation of God's plans for you. He is the only one who can truly help you put the past behind and press on towards the future.

FOR FURTHER REFLECTION

Isaiah 43:18–19
2 Corinthians 5:17

Build on Hardships

*Look at life's difficulties as valuable training for your
character development and for future endeavours.*

Life can be hard sometimes. Perhaps it may seem for some of
us as if it's hard all the time. We would love to think that God's
freedom would mean that affliction would never happen again,
but that is not the case. God never promised that he would completely remove afflictions or hardships from us. What he did
promise is that he would be there to strengthen us and walk with
us through it all. God wants to give us strength in adversity. He
wants to teach us how to thrive and be overcomers, not victims
and survivors of our circumstances. So go to God as your safe
place and refuge and seek his strength in adversity.

FOR FURTHER REFLECTION

2 Corinthians 4:8–9

Maintain Insight

*When you are calm within, you can better
see the order in the chaos.*

A tendency most of us share is to feel responsible for fixing any chaotic situation we find ourselves in and to react by throwing ourselves into it. But chaos can never be fixed if you're a part of it. Chaos can only be fixed if you remain centred and calm and hold onto your inner peace, which will allow you to be more perceptive. If you are internally balanced, you will be able to see things from a bird's-eye view and, when solutions present themselves, you will be able to act on them. The alternative is to become emotionally tangled in the situation, in which case finding solutions will be difficult and acting on them nearly impossible. So maintain a cool head, listen for God's guiding voice and calmly proceed in a spirit of trust and confidence.

FOR FURTHER REFLECTION

Psalm 121:1–2
Colossians 3:15

Let Go of Anger

Do not suffer from your own anger.
The person who has harmed you has already
moved on, so don't let them keep you fuming.

We're all going to be angry at times, but it's not feeling anger that's the problem. The problem comes when we act on those feelings. We need to be in touch with our feelings and take responsibility for them, but we can't allow them to control us. Some people have been upset for so long that they don't even realise they're still harbouring anger. A person who rules their spirit demonstrates self-control, a fruit of the Spirit that's given to us to help us control ourselves. This means that when we feel a certain way, we can choose not to act on it if we know it's against the Word of God.

FOR FURTHER REFLECTION

Proverbs 16:32
Ephesians 4:26–27

Test Your Love

Patience is the mark of true love.

If you want to be happy and make your significant other happy too, you have to learn to have patience in a relationship. Patience in a relationship stands the test of time. Patience is not about overlooking each other's flaws and follies and letting go of them, or sweeping them under the carpet. Patience teaches us to communicate healthily about the differences we see in each other's mannerisms and habits, and helps us to address incompatibilities or even negative behaviour. Patience helps encourage two people to open up and accept each other more willingly. It's a slow process but we have to understand that the objective is not to change each other but to address concerns in a patient and healthy manner.

FOR FURTHER REFLECTION

Ephesians 4:2
1 Corinthians 13:4–8

Don't Waste Energy

No matter how much we worry or fret about something, it never helps the situation.

Worrying is a waste of time because worrying itself is your mind's attempt to deal with an imaginary future situation. Since you can only deal with an event that is happening now, in the present, it's a waste of time to attempt to feel better by thinking about what may or may not happen in the future. When the future situation you're worried about comes into the present, that is when you can actually assess the problem and do something about it, but not a moment before then.

FOR FURTHER REFLECTION

Matthew 6:25
Matthew 6:34

Release the Cares of the Day

Do something serene. Go for a walk,
light some candles, take a bubble bath or
just sit and meditate.

Discover what it is that relaxes you and make that your 'go to' thing after a long day. There is increasing pressure to perform and meet expectations, creating a treadmill of stressful activity day after day. Somewhere along the way society gave up on notions such as relaxation and living in the moment as an important part of daily life. It is easy to be consumed by 'shoulds' and 'musts'. Start to think of your time spent in solitude or engaging in a relaxing activity as an investment in your health, longevity and well-being. The belief that we do not have enough time in the day is a myth that can be unravelled. Just be aware of what consumes your time.

FOR FURTHER REFLECTION

2 Thessalonians 3:16
John 14:27

Internalise Scripture

Memorise a Bible verse that has personal significance to you. Then close your eyes and slowly repeat the verse or a phrase, taking in every word.

Memorising scripture is as an excellent strategy for spiritual growth. It allows you to have gospel truths ready at all times, whether your day brings you temptation, heartache or a friend in need of encouragement. Find a verse in your Bible that inspires you, then read the verse through several times thoughtfully, aloud or in a whisper. This will help you grasp the verse as a whole. Each time you read it, say the topic, reference, verse, and then the reference again out loud.

FOR FURTHER REFLECTION

Psalm 119:11
Colossians 3:16

Choose Your Battles

*If a problem can be solved, there is no need
to worry about it. If a problem cannot be solved,
there is no reason to worry about it.*

Worry is primarily based on fear and uncertainty. It's the anxiety caused when we think we might lose something important to us. You could be worried about losing your job, you could be worried about losing a relationship, or you could be worried you're losing your mind. You could be afraid because you're losing the ability to control a situation; you could be anxious about the future, or you could be afraid of losing a dream. In all these situations, worrying can't influence anything except your own mental health. Worry is not for you, it's against you!

FOR FURTHER REFLECTION

Romans 8:31

Use Your Imagination

*Imagine yourself as a child lying on your back,
gazing into a cloudless sky and blowing bubbles
through a plastic ring. Doesn't that bring a smile?*

When it comes to imagination, children are excellent teachers. They're always wondering about the world: Why is the sky blue? Why do lions roar? What makes the earth spin? An imaginative spirit keeps them open to possibilities and grounds them in the present moment. Is it possible to find that once again? Many great ideas have been come into the world because a believer used their imagination. Just think of what is available to the person who allows the Holy Spirit to form his imagination. The possibilities are limitless!

FOR FURTHER REFLECTION

Ephesians 1:17–18
Mark 11:24

Smile

*Try smiling in the company of others
and see what happens.*

You will be surprised how a smile can trigger the exact same response from someone else. There are many health benefits to smiling – it lowers the stress hormones cortisol, adrenaline and noradrenaline and produces hormones that stabilise blood pressure, relax muscles, improve respiration, reduce pain, accelerate healing and stabilise your mood. But what if you don't feel like smiling? Can you fake it till you make it? Though a heartfelt smile has a deeper effect, even a surface smile tricks the brain into releasing happy hormones.

FOR FURTHER REFLECTION

Proverbs 15:13–14
Job 9:27

Don't Retaliate

If someone behaves angrily towards you,
do not respond with anger.

Anger comes as a result of many causes. The root cause is tension from past hurts and guilt. This mixture of pain and guilt is cumulative and it erupts in anger when new offences remind us of past experiences. Most people assume that hurtful events in the past will be forgotten and will have no effect on the future. That is not true. Past hurts do not just go away, nor does guilt simply disappear after a wrong response to a situation. Unless these experiences are resolved through repentance and forgiveness, we will continue to experience bouts of anger when our tension points are triggered. So if someone behaves angrily toward you, don't put fuel on the fire.

FOR FURTHER REFLECTION

Proverbs 15:1
Proverbs 15:8

Don't Rush

*Overcome the habit of rushing to complete things.
Ask yourself: 'What am I rushing for?'*

It's human nature to want to get a job done as quickly as possible. Getting a task done in a hurry gives you the ability to start your next task sooner. Many of us also grew up being told that it's important to accomplish as much as we can. But what we often aren't told is that rushing can result in accidents, errors and more time spent in the long run. We need to do our jobs correctly and safely. Rushing to get our jobs done can result in injury to ourselves and those around us. The best remedy for suffering the consequences of rushing is to start early. So pace yourself – get to work a few minutes early, plan your day and avoid the constant feeling of being behind.

FOR FURTHER REFLECTION

Proverbs 14:15
Proverbs 21:5

Pray Together

*Form your own prayer group with people
who are willing to team up with you in prayer.
Something special happens when two or more
pray with one accord.*

There's nothing like having someone join you in prayer when together you petition the throne of God over the same matter. It's also comforting when someone comes alongside you, sharing your burden and concern and uniting with you in prayer. Sometimes we may not have the words to pray and need someone else to stand in the gap and pray for us. Forming an ongoing prayer-partner relationship will create a deep connection between you. You'll have someone to open up to and share deeply with, someone to celebrate and share blessings with and someone to care for and pray for.

FOR FURTHER REFLECTION

Matthew 18:19–20

Take Notice

Listen to the sounds of quietness.
Hear the wind murmuring, the leaves rustling,
the birds flapping their wings and your soft breathing.

It's amazing what we can actually hear when we remove the hustle and bustle of everyday noise. Finding a quiet place where we are surrounded by nature allows our hearing to tune into the refreshing sounds we often block out. It gives the mind a break from deciphering the everyday sounds that bombard the brain. Find that golden time of silence today and allow the real sounds of nature to speak to your soul.

FOR FURTHER REFLECTION

Ecclesiastes 3:7–8

Tell the Truth

*Say 'no' when you are asked to do something
you really do not want to do.*

While saying 'no' can be empowering and liberating to some, for others it can be intimidating or uncomfortable. At times society teaches us that the word 'no' is impolite and inconsiderate. We feel obliged to go along with things we honestly do not want to do in order to be socially accepted. However, there are benefits to saying 'no'. It may be a daunting thing to do, but it allows us to choose where we put our time and energy, focusing on the people and parts of our lives that really matter. This is when we'll start to thrive.

FOR FURTHER REFLECTION

Matthew 5:37

DAY 294

Think Before You Act

Do only what you will not regret.

Being quick to hear means listening closely and carefully to what you are being told. Being slow to speak means thinking over things before you open your mouth – that is, making sure your brain is engaged before putting your mouth into gear. Being slow to anger means considering your reaction before taking any action, for anger clouds your judgement. These are important lessons that we can all benefit from.

FOR FURTHER REFLECTION

James 1:19–20

Become Acquainted with Nature

Visit the local park or woods.
Learn the names of the flowers and plants.
Then take time to sit and reflect on nature.

Through nature, God is able to teach us many things. Each plant and flower is unique, providing us with a plethora of amazing names and species. Entering into the world of plants and flowers takes you into a new domain of appreciation of what is right there around you. Learning to identify and call a flower by its name brings greater enlightenment. You will begin to notice the small features of a flower – the shape of its leaves, the arrangement of petals, the size of the stem, the colour of its flower and even the fragrance. Let's discover a new world right in our own vicinity.

FOR FURTHER REFLECTION

Job 12:7–10
John 1:3

Treasure Loved Ones

Remember that your loved ones will one day be gone.
Treasure every precious moment with them.

Cherish your loved ones. You never know when God will call them to sleep. If you've ever experienced the loss of a loved one, the pain can be almost unbearable. For people who don't know the goodness of the love of Jesus Christ, the pain can become too much to handle. But those who know the love of Jesus Christ know that saying goodbye to their loved ones on earth doesn't mean they're saying goodbye for ever. They have the peace and comfort of knowing that they will see their loved ones again. We never know when we will lose someone dear to us, so be fully present with your loved ones while you have the chance.

FOR FURTHER REFLECTION

John 15:12–13

Look After Yourself

God wants the best for your health.
You are the steward of your own body – it's your
temple, so don't put anything into it will defile it.

Being physically healthy enables you to have better overall health, including in your relationships. You only get one body, so taking care of it is important. It's easy to put taking care of yourself on the back burner. With all our family and work responsibilities and everyday demands, self-care can seem like a luxury or even selfish. But taking better care of your mind and body gives you the tools you need to handle life's stresses. Eating well, reducing stress, exercising regularly and taking time out when you need it are touchstones of self-care that help keep you healthy, fit and balanced.

FOR FURTHER REFLECTION

3 John 1:2
1 Corinthians 6:19–20

Take Action

Don't let anger blow up inside you.
Talk to God about what's troubling you and
deflate the balloon before it bursts.

Anger is a complicated emotion and we've all had moments when it's got the better of us. Sometimes, it comes on so fast and strong that it overwhelms us, throwing calm and rational behaviour out of the window. However, we can take a resilient approach to dealing with this complex emotion, as opposed to being controlled by it. It's all about learning to recognise the symptoms of oncoming anger and instead of lashing out, using the energy anger produces to help us find a solution to the problem at hand.

FOR FURTHER REFLECTION

Psalm 37:8
Proverbs 15:1

Be an Instrument of Love

*Love does not come through finding the
perfect person, but by learning to accept an
imperfect person perfectly.*

The Greek word for unconditional love is *agape*. Within its
meaning is the understanding that the person giving love does so
with an understanding that they expect nothing back in return.
There are no conditions or limitations. It's the kind of deep love
that God has for us. When we embrace God's love we allow ourselves to be conduits for that love to reach out and love other
people. It's not a love that naturally flows from us, but we can
learn to love others in this way when we fully understand the
depths of God's love for us.

FOR FURTHER REFLECTION

1 John 4:7–21

Be Assured of God's Presence

*We will never know the full extent of God's
protection over us each and every day. He is an
ever-present companion.*

God watches over us each day. Not in a condemnatory way, waiting for us to slip up and fall, but genuinely to be by our side. If he can notice the sparrow and the fading blade of grass, you know he's tenderly keeping you in mind. We can't see with our physical eyes the spiritual domain that exists, but if we could, we would see a host of God's angels guarding our way. Take comfort – you are never alone!

FOR FURTHER REFLECTION

Psalm 121:5–8

An Undying Love

*God continues to love us even when we go through
phases when we may feel highly unlovable.*

There are days when we will feel unlovable, maybe when we're
feeling low or our self-esteem has taken a hit. It's especially
during these times that we need to be reminded of God's constant loving thoughts toward us. What's important is not what
other people think of you, but what God thinks of you. Get your
validation from his perspective of you and no one else's.

FOR FURTHER REFLECTION

Jeremiah 29:11
Romans 5:8

Let God Lead

*While God's purpose and plan for your life may
be different from others, he is infinitely wise about
the best course of action for you.*

The path that God wants us to travel on will always lead to the best outcome. That's not to say that the journey along the way will be easy. It's just that the final destination will have eternal dividends. God knows your potential and abilities. He has the perfect plan that will enable you to reach your full potential. Let God influence and lead in your decision-making and consult him at every step of the way!

FOR FURTHER REFLECTION

Romans 8:28
Psalm 32:8

Set Yourself Free

Unforgiveness is an umbilical cord that keeps you tied to the past. When you forgive you cut that cord.

Wilful unforgiveness can be dangerous. It will backfire on you. It's different from going through a process of forgiveness where you may have been hurt and need time to work things through. It's when you decide in your heart that you will not forgive that the internal damage takes place. Unbeknown to you, the unforgiveness, which is tied to negative feelings of hatred and anger, will slowly eat away at you. Don't be bound by these destructive feelings – set yourself free and let go of the emotions that keep you captive to a spirit of unforgiveness. You have a brighter future to live and enjoy!

FOR FURTHER REFLECTION

Ephesians 4:32

Believe in Others

Knowing the worst about us, God still sees the best in us.
That's what he expects us to do for others.

Seeing the good in other people may be clouded by our judgements of them based on how they look, talk or walk. Looking beyond these external characteristics and seeing the person beneath is where a true spirit of humanity lies. The external only describes the physical demeanour – the character reveals the true value of the person. If you can bypass your initial impressions of someone and learn to discover their inner beauty, you will be surprised to discover how far your first thoughts were from the truth.

FOR FURTHER REFLECTION

Philippians 2:3

Let God Mould You

*God likes to take the least, the last and the lowest
and make something beautiful of them.*

All the people God chose in the Bible to be leaders had their limitations. Moses was not a good speaker. David was too young. Isaiah felt unworthy. Esther was from a different culture. Nevertheless, God called them. He saw in them something which perhaps they didn't see in themselves – they all had potential to do great things once they depended on God. Each of the leaders mentioned was successful, but not in their own strength, because they knew where they were coming from. God can do great things through you too. If you see yourself as someone who could never lead or form a ministry, then maybe that feeling of unworthiness is exactly what God is looking for in you!

FOR FURTHER REFLECTION

1 Samuel 16:7
Isaiah 43:1

DAY 306

Accept People's Differences

Choosing to love those who are different from you in culture, ethnicity and race is a real challenge to be conquered.

Our natural tendency is to gravitate toward those who share a similar cultural outlook or who look like us. This pattern of behaviour, however, can come at the price of a loss of understanding and appreciation of others who are different from you. We have much to learn from those who are from outside our natural comfort zone of companionship. When you cross that divide, you will be surprised at how much you can learn from differences, but you will also find how much you and others have in common. Learn to appreciate and respect others different from you, to the point that you never consider yourself greater than someone else because of culture, status or education.

FOR FURTHER REFLECTION

John 13:34–35

Be There

*When someone is hurting, words may
fail to bring comfort, but by just being there,
your presence alone speaks volumes.*

When it comes to encouraging someone who is hurting the last thing you should do is talk too much. You may think that saying comforting words and sharing your own personal stories of hurt are beneficial, but usually they're not. Your presence alone speaks louder than any long-winded advice you may give. In fact, the person may not even be focusing on what you say and will probably forget your words. What will not be forgotten, however, is knowing that you were with them in their time of need. So let your words be few. Listen more, talk less and just allow the silent presence of God to be activated through you.

FOR FURTHER REFLECTION

2 Corinthians 1:3–4

Avoid Selfishness

*By nature we are takers, not givers. Try to
reverse that by asking: 'What can I do to serve you?'
rather than: 'What's in it for me?'*

Part of human preservation is survival during times of crisis. If something causes an imbalance in the normality of life our natural response is to ensure we are safe and secure. Sometimes this instinctive behaviour spills over into everyday life. Human nature seeks what's best for itself and this can often be at the expense of others. When others are disadvantaged in order for you to prosper, a deep form of selfishness is exhibited. Jesus gave us the perfect example of how to treat other people. He valued each person, even to the point of showing a servant-leader attitude in washing his disciple's feet. Christ taught that no one should esteem themselves higher than another, and that no one should step over someone else to get to where they want to be.

FOR FURTHER REFLECTION

John 13:1–17
Philippians 2:3–4

DAY 309

Accept Yourself

*To love yourself is not being proud,
but appreciating and accepting who you are in Christ.
Before you can truly love others, you have to
learn to love and accept yourself.*

If you have a low self-image, the likelihood is you will allow this marred view of yourself to cloud how you appreciate and accept other people. The measure by which you judge yourself will be the same measure by which you judge other people. Learning to accept and appreciate who you are with all your flaws and short-comings, believing that you're still a work in progress, will go a long way towards helping you to accept others for who they are. Remember – God has a high estimation of you, so align your thinking with his.

FOR FURTHER REFLECTION

Matthew 22:39
Luke 12:6–7

Be Calm and Carry On

It's when you are in a state of calm that your muscles can relax around your whole body and enable you to think clearly and make important decisions.

The best decisions are made under the influence of a calm mind. This is brought about by diffusing anxious and worrying thoughts and allowing your mind to relax, without the congestion of other things competing for your attention. Weeding out nagging, negative thoughts will allow room for wholesome and refreshing thoughts that will spur on creativity, inspiration and concise decision-making. You will find you are at your most productive when you have fortified your mind with meditation on spiritual thoughts, fresh air, rest and talking to God in prayer. Make these actions a priority and you will see how focused you can be throughout your day!

FOR FURTHER REFLECTION

Song of Solomon 4:1–16

Cherish Precious Memories

Nothing can erase the precious memories you have of a loved one. These treasures belong to you and are to be cherished for the rest of your life.

Treasured memories are developed throughout life's journey. We remember significant things in our lives, but we also remember those seemingly insignificant events that had a profound impact on us. Usually those events involve someone else. When those memories are heart-warming, leading to feelings of happiness, comfort or joy, they become memories you don't ever want to forget. No one can ever take your memories from you, so treasure them as a built-in visual library of special moments in your life and replay them in your mind when you need cheering up.

FOR FURTHER REFLECTION

Psalm 143:5–16
Psalm 9:1

Pray with Love

If love is the greatest emotion in the world and prayer the mightiest force in the world, then imagine what will happen when you combine the two and pray with love for others.

More than ever before, the world needs to see what true love looks like. We can do a lot of good things in this life, like give gifts and even make sacrifices for others. But if we do not have God's love within us, compelling us, filling us, every moment of every day, 'it profits nothing'. God is the author of love because 'God is love'. Therefore all true love emanates from him. When we ask God to fill us with his love, we are asking for the most deep and powerful force known to human nature.

FOR FURTHER REFLECTION

1 John 4:8
1 Corinthians 13:1–7

Look for Open Doors

*Often we look so long at the closed door that we
don't see the one which has been opened for us.*

When one door closes, there's always another door waiting for you to go through. God works way ahead of you. He already knew that before your present door closed, another door was being prepared. Trust God with his direction for your life once you commit it to him. You can be assured that he will never leave you stranded in life. There's always a new path for you to walk down.

FOR FURTHER REFLECTION

Revelation 3:8

Turn It Over

If you hand your problems over to God,
you will experience the power of emotional release,
a very real enhancer of the immune system.

Holding on to your problems will only cause further emotional damage. There comes a release of tension when you can share with someone what you're facing. If you need absolute confidentiality, then talking to God is the best answer. Through prayer, pour out your heart before him. Tell God exactly what's going on. It's not for his information as he already knows, but he wants you to enter into a relationship of trust with him. No problem is so big or so small that God wants you to keep it to yourself. He's the perfect confidant, counsellor and friend.

FOR FURTHER REFLECTION

1 Peter 5:7

Be Open-minded

*We all need to learn not to be quick to judge
or condemn. This means going against our natural
tendency when it comes to judging people.*

We can be easily influenced by what people say about someone or guided by others' opinions. What's important is to press
the reset button, letting go of any preconceived ideas and allowing the true nature of a person to reveal itself. Too often our
judgements are based on false precepts and marred influences.
The best rule is to accept everyone at 100 per cent face value
– that way you're not influenced even by your own prejudices.
It's calming to your soul when you remove all the obstacles that
inhibit accepting a person for who they are.

FOR FURTHER REFLECTION

Romans 14:13
1 Corinthians 4:5
Ecclesiastes 5:2

Give

Giving is the secret of a healthy life.
Giving doesn't just involve money, so be
generous with your encouragement,
sympathy and understanding.

When you give, a wonderful dynamic starts working in your life. You feel you have contributed towards the well-being of someone else. That in itself creates a positive feeling that's released within the body. There's an innate yearning within us to want to help in some way. Harness that desire! Over the generations we have developed a 'what's best for me' attitude where self is placed on the pedestal. You have gifts and qualities within you that, if shared with someone in need, will only help enhance that person's life.

FOR FURTHER REFLECTION

Acts 20:35
Luke 6:38

Claim Your Inheritance

If God is our heavenly Father and we are his children, that makes us all brothers and sisters. We're all from the same family.

We serve one God, whom we call our heavenly Father. We are also given the title of heirs of God and joint heirs with Christ. That makes us royalty. You may never be fortunate enough to have access to the king or queen of your country, but we have direct access to the King of Kings and Lord of Lords. We are a chosen and special people and this title doesn't come to us through privilege or status. It's a position given to all those who are in Christ and who acknowledge God as their heavenly Father.

FOR FURTHER REFLECTION

Romans 8:17
1 Peter 2:9

Find a Secret Garden

*A beautiful garden is a peaceful place
to stop and reflect on life's deeper meaning.
Discover one and be enthralled!*

Away from the hustle and bustle of city life hidden gems of nature can be found. If you live in the country, you will find ample quiet places to reflect on life's meaning. Wherever we live, there are places or retreats we can discover that will lead us to quiet contemplation. It's important to check in with yourself and allow your mind and body to have their say. Find your secret 'go to' place and discover new opportunities to be at peace.

FOR FURTHER REFLECTION

John 18:1

Show Appreciation

Complimenting someone is a wonderful expression of love. Yet compliments are biodegradable – after we receive them they dissolve over time. That's why we always need to refresh our expressions of appreciation.

A compliment is a powerful source of affirmation. It doesn't take much to recognise and appreciate what someone has done. It can be just a simple 'well done' or 'good job', but for the person receiving it, a compliment can go a long way. You have nothing to lose in speaking out empowering words – you have an unlimited storage of such words in your vocabulary. So don't hold back or be reserved about speaking such encouraging words to someone. I guarantee you won't run out of supply, so compliment people unsparingly.

FOR FURTHER REFLECTION

1 Thessalonians 5:11

Find Your Calling

God did not create you to live a purposeless life.
He has a plan just for you. Seek it, find it and live it
to the full.

When you find your calling in life, you find the thing which drives you each day. Your calling is simply what you identify as where you feel God is leading you. If you are unsure what that is, be assured that God delights in you seeking him for direction and guidance in your life. It may be that God's desire is that you simply be the best spouse, father or mother you can be, or to live out your gifts or talents. Either way, God never wants you to believe you don't have an important role to play on earth. Regardless of what anyone says, you are here for a reason and a purpose.

FOR FURTHER REFLECTION

Romans 12:6

Dream Big

*Remember, dreams always come a size too big so
you can grow into them. Don't settle for mediocrity!*

There's no limit to what God can achieve through you. If God is involved, then the outcome will be as big as your faith can stretch. So don't let anyone limit your aspirations. 'If God is for you, who can be against you?' Believe in what God can do through you. He can take the simple things that are in your hands and enlarge and expand them so that they develop into something much bigger than you could think or imagine. So think big, dream big and let God's estimation of what can be achieved filter through to you.

FOR FURTHER REFLECTION

Romans 8:31
Mark 9:23

Let God Surprise You

When things look really bad, remember that
God has surprises up his sleeve that can turn
things around.

When things feel hopeless, don't despair. Never underestimate the power of God. God has more than a thousand ways to provide for us which we don't know about. The beauty of God is that he already knows how things are going to work out. He knows the outcome and he delights in seeing the surprise on our faces when we see the breakthrough, or an open door provided when we thought all the doors were closed. God is able, so wait on him and let him surprise you with unexpected pathways that will bring a smile of awe to your face.

FOR FURTHER REFLECTION

Jeremiah 33:3

Be Transformed

When your situation looks bleak, don't ask
God to take you out of it, but to join you in it.
That way everything is transformed, including you.

Our first tendency when in a difficult situation is to pray for God to remove the problem before us. We want to be released from the heartache, headache or any other ache that the problem causes us. It's only natural to feel this way. We know that the trials of life are there and some hang around for quite a while. Reconfigure your prayers to ask God to journey with you through those moments. It's during the midst of the storm that you need to be assured that God has your back. This assurance will surge through your temporary ordeal and give you the confidence and trust to know that everything's going to be OK.

FOR FURTHER REFLECTION

Mark 4:35–40

Look for the Way Out

Caught in a corner with no way out?
There is a way through.

All of us will feel trapped at some point, whether that is in a job, house, neighbourhood, financial circumstance or relationship. Often feeling trapped can be easily remedied by simply doing something new, but it's not always that easy. However, when we align our lives with God we are promised that a renewal will take place. He enlightens and invigorates us so that we want to learn more of him and grow in character. Feeling trapped is exactly where the enemy wants us to be – in darkness. Let the light of God shine forth, leading to a path that will set you free!

FOR FURTHER REFLECTION

1 Corinthians 10:13
Proverbs 4:18

Turn Weakness to Strength

*When you're at your weakest and most
powerless, that's when God is able to make
you a person of power.*

We all have weaknesses, but it's important to recognise them and ask God to supply his strength for the tasks that lie before us. In times when we feel we can't move forward, we need to remind ourselves that God's grace is sufficient for us. Take courage from our scripture verses today. God has promised us in Romans 8:28: 'And we know that all things work together for good to those who love God, for those who are the called according to his purpose.'

FOR FURTHER REFLECTION

2 Corinthians 12:7–9

Never Walk Alone

Feeling deserted is just that – a feeling.
God makes sure that you are never really deserted.
He is always with you.

Over the course of our lives, there will be times where we are content, surrounded by family and friends. However, the chances are that we will also have times of loneliness where we long for someone to be there with us and support us. The Bible encourages us to be strong and have courage because we are not fighting our battles alone. God is with us no matter what happens, and he won't ever leave or forsake us. He is with us as we walk through all the challenges of life and as we navigate both hard times and good times.

FOR FURTHER REFLECTION

Isaiah 54:10
2 Timothy 4:16–17

Just Call Him

*When we call on God we don't have to go
through security checks. We never get a busy tone,
or get put on hold. He answers the call himself!*

There is no prayer request that is too big, complex or complicated for God to handle. Neither is there any request that is too small, trivial, mundane or inconsequential for God not to give his attention to. God is just a prayer away and he is willing, ready and available to listen to us and answer us when we pray. The question is: are you willing, ready and available to pray?

FOR FURTHER REFLECTION

Psalm 50:15
Jeremiah 33:3

Validate Yourself in Christ

Don't worry about what people think of you –
what God thinks is all that really counts.

Too many of us find ourselves basing our self-worth on how others see us. But it doesn't have to be this way. If only we could see ourselves as God sees us! If we are living to make sure that others love us, we give them permission to evaluate us based on what we do – we give people the power to determine our self-worth. When you feel you don't measure up, accept God's grace and extend it to yourself, knowing that God already sees you as the perfect reflection of Christ.

FOR FURTHER REFLECTION

1 John 3:1–3

Follow God's Way

At a crossroads in life? Check the signposts,
read the map, follow the compass. But above all
talk to the Master Guide.

There are many different times in life when we can find ourselves at a crossroads and feel unsure which way to take. Ultimately, every decision we're faced with is unique and can affect us differently. So it can be difficult to take a leap of faith without knowing exactly how everything is going to pan out. However, if you've found yourself at a crossroads and you're wondering which way to go, then seek godly counsel above all things and let God impress on your mind the path you should take. Then move forward in faith!

FOR FURTHER REFLECTION

Proverbs 3:5–6

Stick with God

Does God seem far away from you?
If so, then someone's moved away, and it wasn't God.

Despite the impressions given about God and his stance towards saving humans, it is not us who run to God – it's God who pursues and runs after us. We simply respond to his bidding and his desire for us to enter into a relationship with him. God has each of us at the centre of his thoughts, as he is not willing that anyone should perish. So assess your relationship with him. If things are going stale for you in your walk with God, ask yourself the question: 'Have I allowed the busyness of life to interfere with my quality time spent with God?' The wonderful thing about God is that he never turns his back on us – he's still there for you.

FOR FURTHER REFLECTION

Psalm 145:18
Psalm 139:7–10

Renew Your Strength

Seven days without prayer makes one weak.

Talking to God on a regular basis is essential for spiritual growth. Without the dynamic of communication, the relationship, like an unexercised muscle, will lose its strength and become weakened. Keeping the relationship alive through prayer is what leads to untold strength and resilience to keep going even in the most trying times. Prayer need not be long and drawn out – it's just having a conversation with God. It involves speaking but also being still, listening to the impressions God wants you to have on your mind. So stay strong and keep the connection alive!

FOR FURTHER REFLECTION

James 5:13–16
1 Thessalonians 5:16–18

DAY 332

Embrace Him

*The Bible's clearest portrait of God is
as a father with outstretched arms running
to give his returning children a hug.*

The story of the Prodigal Son ends with a moving scene where the father runs out to meet his wayward son who has returned home. He then embraces and kisses him, welcoming him back into the family. It's a wonderful image of our heavenly Father, who longs to embrace and welcome back anyone who leaves the fold. God seeks and finds us. He will never abandon or desert us, regardless of what we have done or how low we have stooped. He doesn't want us to live reckless lives, but ones that are in obedience to his will. Nevertheless, that doesn't stop him picking up the pieces of our lives and putting them back together again.

FOR FURTHER REFLECTION

Luke 15:20–24
Luke 19:10

Empty Yourself of Pride

*God gives spiritual food to everyone
except those who are full of themselves.*

When we empty ourselves of pride and selfishness, we will have room for renewal and strength. When you live your life for yourself by maintaining hatred, unforgiveness and discord, this can be likened to an old room full of junk. In order to put new furniture in there, the junk needs to be removed and a spring clean needs to take place to remove stubborn marks, old cobwebs and left-over debris. It all needs to be made new again. That's our life if we have been living it according to our own desires. Only Christ can restore all things to newness. Only he can create in you a clean heart and fill your life with good things.

FOR FURTHER REFLECTION

Psalm 51:10
Proverbs 16:18

Lean on Him

God gives no guarantee that trouble will not strike.
What he does guarantee, however, is to be a tower of
strength in our time of trouble.

We all need someone to lean on in times of need. We may have special people in our lives whom we can go to and call on, but human protection and support will always fall short. Deep within us there is a void that can only be filled by God: a void that yearns for hope, love and a purpose in life. Only God can fulfil those deep, instinctive needs. When we find ourselves in a desperate situation it calls for desperate measures. God says: 'With me all things are possible.' So stick with the one who knows no failure!

FOR FURTHER REFLECTION

Matthew 19:26
Isaiah 43:2–3

Show You Care

The need to be loved is among the deepest cravings of human nature. Let God's love flow through you towards others.

We know God's love is perfect. It has no limits or conditions and is non-partial. It's a love that reaches out to everyone regardless of who we are. Many people are not aware of the depths of God's love for them – that's why he needs you to be his instrument of service. When you allow the love of God to fill you, it can be expressed through random acts of kindness towards others. First you have to be willing to embrace God's love and know that you are special in his eyes. Then with that assurance, let God's love flow out through you in caring acts of kindness.

FOR FURTHER REFLECTION

John 13:34
Romans 12:10

Move Forward in Victory

With God there is no such thing as a mission impossible. When he sends you on a mission he makes sure you have the means to succeed.

When God calls you, he also equips you. This means you can be assured you need not feel you are on your own when it comes to doing something for God. Whether your mission focus is overseas or in your own home, whatever you do for God always has lasting results. When a seed is sown, someone else may water it through another ministry and another may see the plant grow to its full stature. The point is that you have a unique role to play in God's mission field – and when combined with other people's efforts it becomes a universal joint initiative.

FOR FURTHER REFLECTION

1 Corinthians 3:6–8
Luke 1:37

Look for the Light

*Even in our darkest times there are lessons to
be learned and treasures to be discovered.*

When you find yourself in the valley of despondency your faith
is tested to the extreme. When all around you seems dark and
dismal and you can't see any light at the end of the tunnel, that's
when you have to move forward in trust, believing that even
though you can't sense God's presence your faith has to be larger
than going by your feelings. It's in the darkness of your journey
that you have to dig deep into your spiritual reserves and hold on
until you get through to the other side.

FOR FURTHER REFLECTION

Psalm 23:4
John 8:12

Believe That You're Special

There's no way Jesus can ever forget you.
Through his scars from the cross, he carries your
name engraved on the palms of his hands.

Jesus took from this world into the heavenly realms his scars and the nail prints in his hands as a result of dying on the cross. In heaven we will be able to see those nail-scarred hands and know that everything Jesus went through, he went through for me and you. The most amazing thing about Jesus' willing sacrifice is that even if you were the only person in the world, he would have still suffered and died for you. Allow this thought to reinforce in your mind exactly how special and loved you are by God.

FOR FURTHER REFLECTION

Isaiah 49:16
John 3:16

Trust in God

*It's during your anxious times and moments of
weakness that God carries you and your burdens.*

The story of the footprints in the sand brings a vivid image of
Christ carrying us and our burdens as we go through our deepest
struggles. When we look back and see only one set of footprints
in the sand, we will know they were not ours, they were Christ's.
You may never know exactly how you got through life's struggles,
but one thing is for sure, it wasn't through your own strength.
You are only here today because of what Christ has done behind
the scenes in your life.

FOR FURTHER REFLECTION

1 Peter 5:7

Celebrate Your Salvation

God can save from the 'guttermost' to
the 'uttermost' – no one is beyond his reach.

You can't stoop so low in life that God can't find you, pick you up and plant your feet on a solid foundation. You may know someone who feels wretched and unworthy. They feel there is no hope and that they have transgressed too far for God to have any mercy on them. Let them know that there is hope – that God's mercy extends far beyond our human understanding. Assure them that their life is still full of potential because God never leaves us in a heap. God is in the businesses of restoration.

FOR FURTHER REFLECTION

Hebrews 7:25

Keep Your Chin Up

Overcoming rejection starts with understanding
and accepting how much God loves and values you.

We live in a world where people can be very cruel. Because evil abounds, we see the effects of it played out in the lives of people who take advantage of each other, put others down and will reject you in order to enhance their own prospects. Don't allow other people's negative estimations of you to be your criteria for self-evaluation. Look beyond other people's negative comments and rise above the low level they would want to place you at. Your value as a person is of inestimable worth.

FOR FURTHER REFLECTION

1 John 3:1

Trust the Process

God has a plan for your life.
It includes things you can't have today,
but will be able to enjoy tomorrow.

Deferred gratification is not something we generally like. Instant gratification is what we have become used to. It's played out in fast food, next-day delivery and instant fixes – we want everything now! Unfortunately this attitude has crossed over into the spiritual realm. We want our prayers answered immediately, our trials to end overnight and God to show up when we ask him. God understands all of this, but he doesn't work according to our timetable. He works according to the best timing for us. Because he knows all things, trust him with the process.

FOR FURTHER REFLECTION

Psalm 37:7

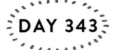

Accept God's Way

Through what you're experiencing right now,
God is developing qualities in you that can't be
developed in any other way.

You may not realise it, but even now, as you go through whatever it is you're dealing with, you're learning new things about yourself. New character traits that were previously hidden will come to the fore when certain buttons have been pushed in your life. It's through the challenges and hardships of life that you discover things about yourself that you never thought existed. These new aspects of your character may reveal that, deep down, you have greater strength and resolve than you realised.

FOR FURTHER REFLECTION

2 Corinthians 4:16–18

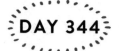

Let God Decide

*God knows what's right for you. If something is right,
he will provide it. If it's not, he will give you
something better.*

God knows best. Yet often we question his choice and the
process. God is not fazed if we challenge or question him. He
expects us to enter into a dialogue with him about how things
are panning out in our lives. However, God does want us to trust
him. The basis of that trust is the belief that God only wants the
best for us. If he sees that giving us something will turn out to
be harmful or will draw us away from him, then God will steer us
away from that. It's about learning to believe that God's thoughts
and understanding are way off the scale compared to ours. If
you don't get want you want, know this – God has something in
store for you that in time will make what you originally wanted
so insignificant that you will be relieved it wasn't granted.

FOR FURTHER REFLECTION

Matthew 7:11

See the Beauty Within

When God made you, he didn't just decorate the outside. He gave you inner beauty – the gentle, gracious kind he delights in.

Inner beauty is what God sees. Unfortunately most people only look at the outward display of who we are. We can easily miss out on getting to know someone better simply because there's a failure to look beyond their outward appearance. It behoves us to see people as God see them – as children of God whom he loves infinitely. When you begin to see people in the way God sees you, then there will be no room for misguided views or assumptions about someone based on first impressions.

FOR FURTHER REFLECTION

1 Peter 3:4
2 Corinthians 4:16

Draw Closer

The extent to which you consciously lean on God and his strength is the extent to which you will lower your anxiety level.

We need to lean on God when life is overwhelming because he is our strength, our lifeline and the one who directs our steps. We need to lean on him when we don't have the answers, when the mountain we need to be moved doesn't move, when the flood waters rise and it seems as if there is no way out. We desperately need him. We need his presence and his peace. We need him to be our refuge and our shield when life is hard, to get us through those days when we just want to give up. The good thing is that whenever we need him, he is always there.

FOR FURTHER REFLECTION

James 4:8
Jeremiah 29:12–14

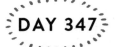
Think Things Through Clearly

The truth is, life is ten per cent what happens to you and ninety per cent how you respond to it.

We have all heard the famous saying above. In life, attitude is everything – it is what shapes our beliefs and our desires. Harsh times will occur throughout our lives, but it is up to us how we interpret them. Many people blame their circumstances for their shortcomings. Such people believe an event is equivalent to its outcome – however, for the person who depends on God, adversity is where they thrive. The less you start blaming your unfavourable circumstances and the more you start determining how you will react and respond, the better life will be for you.

FOR FURTHER REFLECTION

Philippians 4:11–12

Stay in the Game

Each time you fall, there's a moment of decision –
you can either give up or get up and persevere
through to victory.

People who trust in the Lord and depend on God throughout their lives may trip and fall over and over again, but they won't stay down. They will overcome obstacles and challenges by God's grace and strength, dusting themselves off and rising again. Resilience is one of the blessings of those who choose right living because God is on their side. 'The steps of a good man are ordered by the Lord, and he delights in his way. Though he fall, he shall not be utterly cast down; for the Lord upholds him with his hand' (Psalm 37:23–24).

FOR FURTHER REFLECTION

Isaiah 40:31

Stimulate the Brain

There are centres in the human brain that
respond positively to prayer, reading and meditating
on God's word – light up those brain areas!

Practising a personal religious faith is the most powerful way to maintain a healthy brain. The brain's frontal lobe is used in focusing attention, rational thinking and decision-making. It responds to prayer and meditation by helping to reduce stress, strengthen our immune system, enhance our memory and increase our capacity for compassion. It helps us ward off age-related brain deterioration and live longer. Prayer and reading scripture also deactivates areas in the brain associated with anger, guilt, anxiety, depression, fear, resentment and pessimism. So stimulate the brain with prayer and meditation.

FOR FURTHER REFLECTION

Psalm 139:14

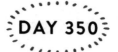

Express Love

Three little words people never get tired of hearing are: 'I love you.' It's not complicated – it just requires thought and consideration.

One of the greatest gifts God gives us are special people who are placed in our lives. These may be family or special friends, but they are there for a reason – to enhance our lives. Our responsibility is to treasure those relationships. We know that life is fleeting and before long those loved ones will have moved on. Use the limited time of your journey in life to ensure your loved ones know they are loved. Actions may speak louder than words, but when it comes to expressing your love, words take on a deeper meaning. Shower love on those whom God has blessed you with. Tell them you love them – let them hear it. Don't reserve the words: 'I love you' for special occasions.

FOR FURTHER REFLECTION

1 Samuel 20:17
Jeremiah 31:3

Share God's Goodness

You're here to be light, bringing out the God-colours in the world. God is not a secret to be kept.

When you know you have been blessed by God, you won't be able to keep your appreciation to yourself. It will be something that you will naturally want to share with those around you. When people are expressing their joy at their football team winning a match, or telling you about the exciting time they had at a concert, they don't hold back. Yet when it comes to expressing joy at what God has done, there's hesitancy. God looks to us to be his mouthpiece – to be his salt and light in a world searching for meaning. Let the beauty of Jesus shine through to others.

FOR FURTHER REFLECTION

Matthew 5:13–14

Be Thankful in All Things

Don't make it difficult for people to please you.
When they see a positive, appreciative response,
it spurs them on to doing it again.

The Holy Spirit in us is what allows us to be thankful even when things aren't going right, to have peace when life feels chaotic, and to have hope when all seems hopeless. When we can't think of anything to be thankful for, the Holy Spirit reminds us that we can be thankful for Jesus – for the forgiveness of sins, for a relationship with God and for the promise of eternal life. Often thankfulness does not come easily. No matter how bad life seems, we have the ability to be thankful. We don't have to thank God for our problems, but we can thank him for the strength he's building in us through them.

FOR FURTHER REFLECTION

1 Thessalonians 5:16–18
James 1:17

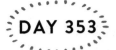

Don't Tense Up

Most of our headaches are of physiological and emotional origin, caused by tight muscles in the neck and shoulders, changes in blood supply and tensions that develop due to the pressures of life.

When we're under pressure, it's important to realise that if we are not careful, it could have an adverse effect on our health. Most importantly, we should use those situations to learn to rely on God. How do we do that? Pray: 'Lord, help me. I need your wisdom and strength!' Continue to trust God when things are beyond your control. Believe that God can bring victory out of seeming defeat. Continue to obey God's revealed will and his clearly expressed commands, and be courageous.

FOR FURTHER REFLECTION

Psalm 118:5–6
Exodus 14:14

Eat Your Apples

An apple a day is said to 'keep the doctor away'.
Apples contain pectin, which lowers the level of
cholesterol and eliminates toxins from the body.
Apples are invaluable!

God has given you the gift of your body and it comes with an owner's manual – the Bible. In it are all the instructions you need to take care of yourself and live a long life. You already know the basics: proper nutrition, exercise, a good night's rest. Apples and many other fruit and vegetables are life and soul for the body. However, you can have all the right macrobiotics and organic food, but if your body is filled with resentment, worry, fear, lust, guilt, anger, bitterness or any other emotional disease, it's going to shorten your life.

FOR FURTHER REFLECTION

Proverbs 17:22
Proverbs 16:24

It Pays to Trust

*God knows everything about you and will richly
reward the trust you place in him.*

We are always told to have faith and to trust God. In certain situations, that is easier said than done. We sometimes think things will be easier if we take matters into our own hands. Nobody ever said having faith would be easy, but it will be worth it and here is why – God knows everything we are going through at this very moment and everything we will go through in the future. He knows the best way to handle every situation so that we will get the best possible outcome and we need to trust him with that.

FOR FURTHER REFLECTION

James 1:6

Treasure Good Friends

There are no better friends than the loyal friends
on whom we can depend, who give us their allegiance
and are constant to the end.

Who is the first person you call when you receive exciting news? Whose shoulder do you cry on when your heart is broken? Who makes you laugh? Who brings you ice cream when you are stressed, or coffee when your newborn had you up all night? We all need faithful friends, but they are few and far between. However, you can become a faithful friend by letting faithfulness stem from you. Remember that ultimately Jesus is the only one who can satisfy the soul.

FOR FURTHER REFLECTION

Proverbs 18:24

Shed That Tear

*Each little teardrop cleanses and helps us understand,
there's wisdom in each trial and pardon in each plan!*

Sometimes we cry because life's sorrows have become chronic. At other times we cry because of some unexpected misery which has carved a crater in our soul. And sometimes we cry and don't know quite why; our grief evades description and analysis. To such mourners, the Bible's message is not to dry up your tears. No – the Bible says weeping is typical of life in the valley and its message to mourners is much more sympathetic. The God of all comfort keeps watch over your weeping. He gathers up all your tears and puts them in his bottle.

FOR FURTHER REFLECTION
Psalm 56:8
Psalm 30:5

Take a New Direction

Failing isn't unusual – it's part of the learning curve.

Mistakes give us a chance to adapt and move on. At times, we're heading in the wrong direction and we just don't know it. So making a mistake can be a learning experience to teach us about the task we're working on – whether it's the way we interact in a relationship or the way we handle customers in a business. It allows us to adapt ourselves to our environment and the people whom we interact with. Making a mistake gives us an opportunity to avoid a wall and move to another path.

Philippians 3:13
Proverbs 9:9

Re-evaluate What's Important

*Once you know that your real identity and worth are
not linked to the car you drive, the size of your house,
your income or your educational background,
it changes your outlook on life.*

Some of the most prosperous people in the world are those who have very little material wealth. Their identity is not related to their status in society, but rather to how they value themselves based on God's perspective. Most happy people know how to make the best of what they have and appreciate the people around them. When you choose to believe God's opinion of you rather than the negative views other people may have, you have moved beyond the trivial to that which is of higher worth and value. That's how God wants you to see yourself – as a person of inestimable worth!

FOR FURTHER REFLECTION

Psalm 139:13–15
Ephesians 4:32

Wait for the Outcome

The crisis you're facing maybe a blessing in disguise;
an opportunity to experience a greater degree of
God's power at work in your life.

We often encounter disappointments that perplex and bother us, and we're tempted to cry out: 'O Lord, why do you allow these things to happen?' But at times like this we should cast ourselves on God's mercy and love. Even though our present trials may be heart-breaking, the all-wise heavenly Father works through them to bring about our ultimate good. We can thank God for our disappointments because they are blessings in disguise!

FOR FURTHER REFLECTION

2 Corinthians 4:16–17
Romans 8:28

Claim God's Mercy and Grace

Others may give up on you, but not God – nothing you've done is beyond the scope of his grace.

God will never abandon you, even when you may have given up on yourself! The name given to God's unfailing patience and commitment to us is mercy, which means not getting what we deserve. Then there is God's grace, which means getting what we don't deserve. Mercy and grace go hand in hand. Between them we are covered in all circumstances. Think about it – the only reason why we are here is because God has been merciful to us despite our sinful condition, and we are blessed each day because God simply loves us too much.

FOR FURTHER REFLECTION

Psalm 40:1–5

Stick with God's Plan

It's in your times of testing that you discover God is faithful. He will stretch you, but never beyond your breaking point.

In order for our faith to grow, it has to be stretched. In order for it to be stretched, we have to exercise it. For our faith to be exercised, we have to go through situations in life that will challenge our existing faith. If that doesn't happen then, like a wasted muscle, faith will deteriorate and become ineffective. So remember – as tough as it might be sometimes, the test you are presently going through will only make you stronger, wiser and, more importantly, closer to God!

FOR FURTHER REFLECTION

1 Peter 1:7
Psalm 119:71
1 Corinthians 10:13

Be Proactive

You don't have to wait until you have high blood pressure to take up a healthy lifestyle. Get into a good exercise regime from now on and start adding quality years to your life.

We have only one shot at life. That means we really have to learn things fast and benefit from our past mistakes and experiences to get ahead in life. If we know that looking after our body, which is the temple of God, is our responsibility, then we need to do what's in our power to ensure only the best enters our body through what we eat and drink, avoiding anything that's harmful. Maintain your health now, rather than waiting for some malady to come upon you before you realise you need to do something about it. Do it now, don't wait.

FOR FURTHER REFLECTION

3 John 2
1 Corinthians 10:31

Wait for the Outcome

The problem you've encountered is not there to stop you – it's there to prepare you. The challenge is not going to defeat you; it's going to prosper you.

Sometimes people mistakenly think that after their salvation, God is going to make life comfortable and stress-free, but that's not what scripture promises. Trials are designed by the Lord to test our faith, humility, submission and values. We can either waste our difficulties by defiantly resisting God or benefit by trusting in and depending on him. The first way leads only to suffering, but the second option results in spiritual maturity and eternal rewards. With a positive attitude and a humble and submissive heart, wait and see what God wants to accomplish in your life.

FOR FURTHER REFLECTION

John 16:33
1 Peter 4:12
James 1:2

Be a Blessing

Start a blessing! Make your life count.
You can affect generations of people just by your
influence, so as you are blessed, become a blessing
and start changing lives a moment at a time!

God's blessings don't terminate with you, but travel onwards. You are simply a conduit for God's blessings to flow on to someone else. It's amazing how you can subtly have an impact on another person. You may not even be aware of it – sometimes it's just your demeanour or attitude that someone picks up and learns from. We all play a role in bringing about change. Sometimes the only way God can reach someone noticeably is through you. So be blessed and be a blessing!

FOR FURTHER REFLECTION

2 Corinthians 9:8
Matthew 5:16

Walk by Faith

You have to believe when there is no sign.
Just because you don't see anything happening on
the outside, it doesn't mean something is not
happening on the inside.

Society almost demands that seeing is believing. To some extents it is, but in the spiritual realm where faith becomes an important factor, not everything is revealed to us. God in his wisdom knows when to reveal his handiwork so that we can see it with our own eyes. The true test of faith, however, is learning to walk by faith and not by sight. This means taking God at his word, believing in his promises and trusting God in the process of waiting. So keep on the path of faith and ask God to develop within you 'inner sight' to see by faith what has yet to be revealed to human eyes.

FOR FURTHER REFLECTION

2 Corinthians 5:7
2 Kings 6:17-20

Acknowledgements

For the support and encouragement given to me during the process of this book, I give thanks and appreciation to my family: my wife Maxine and three boys, Ryan, Simeon and Liam.

It has also been a long and joyful journey working with William Collins and HarperCollins, and I thank the team of editors for their vision and belief in me in producing yet another book that is designed to help make a difference in people's lives.

Other books by Richard Daly

Available at http://harpercollins.co.uk

Notes

....

....

....

....

....

....

....

....

....

....

....

....

....

....

....

....

....

Notes

Notes

....

....

....

....

....

....

....

....

....

....

....

....

....

....

....

....

....

....

Notes

....
....
....
....
....
....
....
....
....
....
....
....
....
....
....
....
....
....
....

Notes

....
....
....
....
....
....
....
....
....
....
....
....
....
....
....
....
....
....
....

Notes